Polished Stones

Enjoy
Elizabeth Wesley

Dedicated to:

Heidi and Ben
&
Robert and Tracey

Elizabeth Wesley
ew33l55e77w@gmail.com

authorHOUSE®

AuthorHouse™
1663 Liberty Drive
Bloomington, IN 47403
www.authorhouse.com
Phone: 1-800-839-8640

© 2011 by Elizabeth Wesley. All rights reserved.

No part of this book may be reproduced, stored in a retrieval system, or transmitted by any means without the written permission of the author.

First published by AuthorHouse   12/05/2011

ISBN: 978-1-4634-2001-7 (sc)
ISBN: 978-1-4678-7152-5 (hc)
ISBN: 978-1-4634-2000-0 (ebk)

Library of Congress Control Number: 2011909811

Printed in the United States of America

Any people depicted in stock imagery provided by Thinkstock are models, and such images are being used for illustrative purposes only.
Certain stock imagery © Thinkstock.

This book is printed on acid-free paper.

Because of the dynamic nature of the Internet, any web addresses or links contained in this book may have changed since publication and may no longer be valid. The views expressed in this work are solely those of the author and do not necessarily reflect the views of the publisher, and the publisher hereby disclaims any responsibility for them.

Introduction

There are poems that seek
And some that keep;
Troubles that we find.
But some are fun,
They bring the sun
And help to heal the mind.
For things that are spoken
Find hearts that are broken,
Needing words to heal;
But joy can be found
If we let words surround,
Thoughts we can't conceal.
So it's time to look,
Turn the pages of this book
And find where reason leads;
For words can say
All that brightens the day,
To give the mind what it needs.

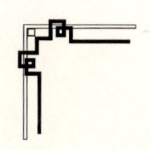

Moonlight Magic

The night was fickle as November
A time when all sleep in slumber;
The moist mist hangs over the river,
And a still cold moon hangs as a sliver.

A soft liquid light captures the glow,
Of the first few flakes of new fallen snow;
She shines her light on turret towers,
And tucks in bed the sleeping flowers.

Her crescent rides through clouds that fly,
Shining on wolves as they howl and cry.
Etching the transient phantoms of night,
As wings of an owl brush the dust of flight;

The crystalline light shines on lovers,
Yet pale and still the moonlight hovers;
To tip with silver the restless waves,
And on tombstones marking silent graves.

Cast your moonbeams, cast them down,
As you float in your silver crown;
And the ribbon of dawn will wrap your head,
And put your shining eye to bed.

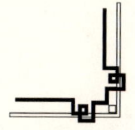

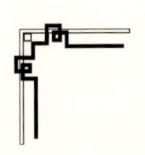

The Ride

He mounted his horse impatient to ride,
With silver spurs and a heavy stride;
The clatter of hooves on the cobblestone street,
Flew on limbs so swift and fleet.
The moon rose above the copse on the hill,
Casting dark shadows gloomy and still;
The clock chimed twelve in the village square,
As he rode through the street shrouded and bare.
The toll of the bell in the stone church tower,
Rang long and loud at the midnight hour.
The moon rose above the graves on the hill,
Casting dark shadows dim and still;
Beneath the churchyard lay those who died,
But still he rode on with measured stride.
A glimmer of light from the belfry's height,
Pierces the gloom of the cold dark night;
As he leans in the saddle with reigns in his hand,
With flying feet he gallops over the land.
Ride up the hill and down in the dale,
His cape flying in the wind like a serpent's tail;
He rode his horse faster and fleet,
With sparks flying out from under his feet;
And people rose from their beds to listen and heed,
Of the footfall of rider and his gallant steed.

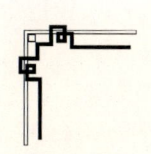

March

The footfall of March comes whistling by,
Wrapped in the hope that winter will die;
But the winds of winter still coldly blow,
Bringing the harvest of leftover snow.

The birds from south wing their way home,
From faraway places where feathered wings roam;
Pregnant with the breathless feelings that bring,
Promises of hope in the womb of Spring.

The bright days of Eden are almost here,
Blossoms that are sleeping will soon appear;
But only the snowdrop lifts her brave little head,
From a cold dank earth and lonely bed.

But the skies of grey are turning blue,
The days grow longer and storms are few;
Earth has joys to bring in her arms,
As the birth of Spring brings in all of her charms.

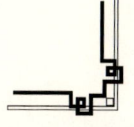

June

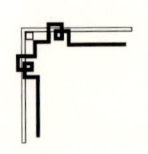

The languid eyes of soft sleepy June,
Awaken to tease the flowers that bloom;
With liquors of dew for striped honey bees,
Dipping their straws if the blossom agrees.

Let the whispering wind fly with no haste,
Thro pavilions of blossoms dotted with lace;
Where tender feet trip thru the myriad of greens,
To paint the pastures of June's sunny scenes.

The ancient forests deck far away hills,
Where winding streams drift thru unruly rills;
And the alchemy of all that is told,
Turns mossy stones into precious gold.

The perfumed petals adorned with scent,
Surround everywhere the elfin spirits went;
As these little ones skipped thru the sunlit day,
It was with these shadows I needed to play.

So the chapter of June comes to a close,
She floats into summer on the scent of a rose;
She pirouettes on tiptoe in her gossamer gown,
Wearing on her head a bright golden crown.

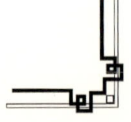

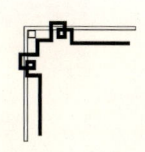

Pilgrims without Progress

Pilgrims without progress were a people by name,
They travelled a road that was always the same.
The way that was mapped for the route they took,
Was inscribed by pen in a leather bound book.

The road was rocky and scattered with thorn,
And the people were hot and feeling forlorn.
Their feet were sore and their faces were red,
And the sun shone without mercy down on their head.

The distance was painted with bright coloured flowers,
That soothed the eye and filled the long hours;
And a hawk that soared high in a bright blue sky,
Was looking for food to feed her babies nearby.

They kept on walking throughout the dark night,
With the moon on high shining her light.
A breeze that comforts touched their weary face,
Urging them onward to finish the race.

Though travels of all made them weary and sore,
A need to get there was not helping anymore;
For the way that they went led all of them round,
Back to the place where the beginning was found.

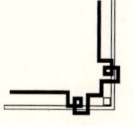

Waiting for You

Daylight is dying
Twilight comes flying
Purple and crimson blaze in the sky;
The sun's in a rush
To fade with a flush
And kiss the meadow good bye.

An hour for trysting
When you come unresisting
Precious and eager on hesitant feet;
Shadows disguise us
Rose scent to baptize us
Scenting our bed with odours so sweet.

We can't know the reason
Or the span of a season
But eternal the stars shine up above;
We never had sought it
We never had thought it
Were it not jeweled with the beauty of love.

But all is forgiven
By chance that has given
An hour for the transition of youth;
We never will know it
But our dream will now show it
Changing it all to astonishing truth.

The fireflies ignite you
My breath will excite you
Nothing will vex the passing of hours;
Come, I await you
Night is too late for you
Come while the dewdrops are kissing the flowers.

The wind of the night is
Fragrant with lilies
Touched by the scent, kissed by the dew;
The garden lies breathless
Where love awaits deathless
Under the starlight, I'm waiting for you.

Camelot

There was a camel that trots a lot,
He trotted his way from Camelot;
With tasseled fringe and jeweled saddle,
He forded the sea with a golden paddle;
Up the dunes and across the sands,
He traversed the way to Arab lands;
Where there is no water to pump,
So he carried it in his camel's hump.

On the way from Camelot,
The rider found that he forgot
All the jewels and precious things,
Borrowed with haste from Hottentot kings;
So he turned his camel around,
For what was lost had not been found.
Then he steered his beast toward the east,
Where men of China drink and feast.

The man who came from Camelot,
Sat on his camel and smoked some pot;
He puffed with need on the evil weed,
Till his lungs were filled with empty greed.
He spent his days looking glazed,
And what he smoked caused some delays;
But the man on the camel that liked to trot,
His name of fame was Sir Lancelot

Now Sir Lancelot was very hot,
And he never found a shady spot;
But he had a drink from the camel's hump,
By using his hand to pump the lump.
And all the while the camel was panting,
While Sir Lancelot was loudly ranting;
And the words he spoke were poppycock,
All the way back to Camelot.

Do You Love Me

Do you love me enough, am I dear,
Do you hold me most precious of all?
In the quiet spaces of your heart,
Do you make it known, is it clear
To the one you love? If death's quick call
Should suddenly tear us apart
Leaving no time for a sad farewell,
Would you feel you had nothing to tell
Of things you wish you had said before?
Could you have said more?

Do you love me enough? How swift the years fly,
Faster and suddenly they fade away;
And each one carries its dead
With no words left when we cry.
Soft words to be whispered another day
May never be done or said.
Speak softly to me in my listening ear,
And know I want you to be always near.
Don't wait till I go to the grave,
For the time to tell of love is brief;
But long is the silence of our grief;
Do you love me enough to be brave?

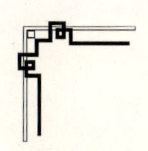

Another Man's War

You won't be here when the lilacs bloom,
You won't breathe their sweet perfume;
Instead my love, you'll follow your star,
To fight with passion another man's war.
Skimming the air, the swallows fly low,
Over the battle where patches of snow
Mingle with mud and stains of blood,
Reaping the tide of that bitter flood.
On foot, by air or by lethal machine,
The fight of war is vast and mean;
Our sons charge thru the valley of death,
Crying aloud with their last breath;
And it plucks the soul and tears the heart
And grieves the loved at home apart.
Both pray to God for His will to win,
In spite of the fact that war is sin;
But love our neighbor and all mankind,
Would heal the loss and mend the mind.

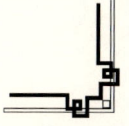

Gypsy Dance

Climb up the hill where gypsies hide,
And breathe on the wind of a restless tide;
Where notes of sorrow from a violin,
Cry out to the night from a heart within.

The day is dim and night is alive,
And gypsies dance like bees in a hive;
They spin and turn while the fire burns bright,
And sparks fly up to kiss the night.

Old men sit while weaving a tale,
While young men sit drinking their ale;
And fires of night flicker and glow,
While the winds of night moan and blow.

They dance too fast, they dance too far;
They follow the light of a fallen star;
But there in the sky a sickle shaped moon,
Dances with gypsies in the fires of June.

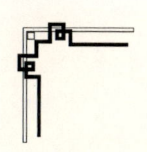

Queen of Hearts

There she sits with grace, and dainty
Satin dressed, a charming lady;
Her dark blue eyes and golden tresses,
Adorns a face that heaven blesses.
Gems and jewels shining, gleaming,
As the queen of hearts sits there dreaming;
Where she sits in lonely fashion,
Not fit to share her only passion
Of love for kings and love for jewels,
Not to mention her share of fools.

The king of hearts comes for his lady,
Down the path neath trees so shady;
Over hill in stately fashion,
Rides the king with all his bastion.
Drums are beating, trumpets blowing,
With the horses onward going;
Down the street on feet that clattered,
As if the dream was all that mattered;
There to meet his blue eyed lover,
A prized illusion to discover;
And all the joy that rang from rafter,
Was nothing more than daydream's laughter.

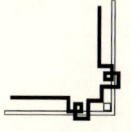

Finger of Fate

Women of wit are treacherous tools,
Ever fatefully embracing idiot fools;
When pleasure waves a finger, it's never too late,
To enjoy the indulgence of the finger of fate.

To tread through briars and hedges of thorn,
Where whimsies shrewd fickle feet are borne;
Tasting with delight the pleasures of pain,
Where everything's lost, and there is no gain.

Whenever a woman of wit should arrive,
Collect your wits to stay alive;
For you know she'll gather her skirts to chase,
And a fickle finger of fate might just save your face.

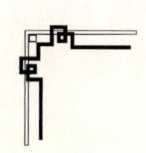

Eden

In the garden two were conceived,
The man and wife were Adam and Eve;
These two who sinned received no pardon,
In fair Eden's perfect garden.

They had a choice to choose from which tree,
But chose the wrong and had to flee,
For the serpent offered a deadly delight,
That was wasted in the garden that night.

This first sin was a vain endeavor,
Resulting in separation forever;
From a God who gave all He could give,
So others who followed could happily live.

Man's disobedience brought much pain,
It took the sun and brought the rain;
Where forbidden passions burned the soul,
And broke in pieces all that was whole.

The days of Eden were dim and cold,
Harboring a lesson that must be told;
We need the truth to help us see,
And that is the secret to keep us free.

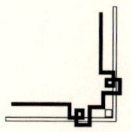

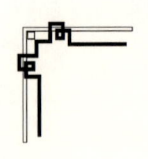

A Summer Afternoon

Summer comes all clothed in green,
To paint the path of a passing scene.
Wheat in the field bound in sheaves,
Shares the glory of gold tipped leaves.

Gossamer drops of morning dew,
Lie on a bed of radiant blue;
And clusters that hang on wandering vines,
Brings juice that gives sweet scented wines.

The midnight owl takes her rest,
Hidden in the tree in a secret nest;
And raucous rooks in ferny nooks,
Take in the scene with cautious looks.

The hawk that flies under sapphire skies,
Stretches her wing till daylight dies;
Poised in flight, her arabesques,
Soaring, dipping, seem so effortless.

Prisms of sunbeams shimmer with gold,
To capture the warmth till day grows old;
Erasing the shadows that go at noon,
As day wastes away, all too soon.

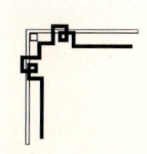

Indian Summer

Memories of autumn linger still
The pale sun loiters on the hill;
A prodigal year now grown old
Is gathering all her days of gold.
Flocks of birds now eager to go
We share the dream with footsteps slow;
We meet beneath the apple tree
Join hands in silent company.
We will not part love, oh not yet
Too soon the weary sun will set.

The crickets cease to sing their song
The gold and russet wilt away;
The crimson trees stayed too long
And all the sky is wet and grey.
We know at night the frost will fall
And scar the asters on the hill;
The golden rod and sumac all
Will feel the hand of winter's chill.

But love, it is not time to part
I need to hold you near my heart;
Yesterday was such a golden smile
Tonight we might love awhile;
Till autumn dies and love forget
When we must leave, but dear not yet.

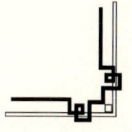

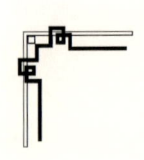

The Hanging Tree

My cup of wine was ruby red,
I ran fast my love to see;
With a heart full of joy I said,
"How wild with love can a man be"?
The stars were laughing overhead,
And I danced with shadows merrily.

I thought, in a week we'll wed,
No more lonesome lady she;
We'll lie together in a bed,
And I will father babies three.
So dancing on the air I sped,
To her who did not wait for me.

Then I went with careful tread,
With beating heart my lass to see;
To the window where the light was shed,
Softly shining on the lea.
Then with my eyes I saw with dread,
Two shadows silhouetted there to see.

Another man sat on the bed,
And she unclothed upon his knee;
She looked in my eyes with dread,
Then her paramour was wont to flee.
Now the floor is bloody red,
And I'm waiting for the hanging tree.

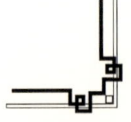

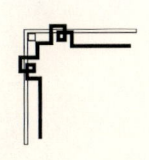

Lullaby

Sleep my darling, the darkness is here,
Floating soft on crystalline dreams;
Scented with perfumes of night so dear,
With starlight sprinkling all of your dreams.
The hooty owl calls his amorous song,
Blessedly silent is the noise of day;
The stars of the night have shown,
Sleep my baby as long as you may.

Sleep my darling, the night is tranquil,
Moonbeams surround you at rest;
The wind is softly calling to you,
With hymns that are ancient and blessed.
Daisies come hither in the field to dance,
Morning comes quickly with tomorrow's tears,
But tonight is star struck with romance,
Sleep my baby with no more fears,
Daylight will come in a couple of years.

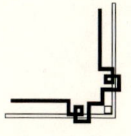

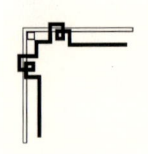

Emily

I forgive you dear Emily,
For you are more than fair;
Your flirty eyes give promise,
Your pouty lips don't care.
From the tilt of your head,
A heart it could break;
Your silken cheek with blush,
Where pretty dimples wake.
The mayhem in your eyes,
That will not look at me;
There the damage lies,
There for all to see.
You wink coquettish lash,
To entice me in the night;
Would the knowing of your heart,
Make everything alright?
What your callous lips may say,
Your naughty eyes deny;
What a tease dear Emily,
Enough to make me cry.

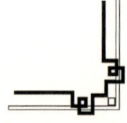

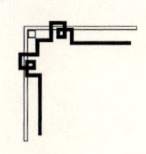

Horseback Ride

I rode down yonder cobbled street,
On stones that clattered 'neath my horse's feet;
Till we reached a grand lampstand,
That marks the place that ends the land
Where city street meets country lane,
And horses ride in summer's rain.

Out on the lane with fleet of foot,
We rode a path within the wood;
To wander round bright green trees.
With ruffled mane in a prodigal breeze,
To spy where pale narcissi lay,
And sparrows decked each floral spray.

Where squirrelly clowns cast their spell,
And twining vine where birdsongs tell
Of all the faerie tales when told,
Were all the joys and tears of old,
That lend their gold to aspen leaves,
And flutter gently in the breeze.

Sunbeams shaft thro trees with light,
Taking shadowed wings in feathered flight.
Along a path the sweet primrose,
Nod their heads with crowns of gold;
And as we leave the woods behind,
Meadowsweet's not hard to find.

From out the shade and into sun,
I urge my horse to a steady run;
Clip clop, clip clop the steady beat,
Defines the rhyme of horse's feet.
She shakes her mane and lifts her tail,
And the light in her eye can never fail.

Through dappled meadow and rutted lane,
We trot the copse through fields of grain;
Where bridal veil of blossoms bloom,
And scent the air with faint perfume.
As we round the corner and take the bend,
Home's right there, we've reached the end.

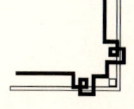

The Dream

From the mouth of the ocean and the eye of the wave
You erupt in my being and leap from my grave;
A lover so gloomy, yet dreadfully bright
You're clothed with the darkness but crowned with light.
You come in the spark, you soar with the fire
The mist is your pillow, the tornado your choir;
I will kiss you to sleep on the wild ocean's crest
A sleeping volcano, an earthquake at rest.
When you feel the earth move under your feet
The sun will bathe you with her sultry heat;
Let not the stars dim the light in your eyes
Let not my passion find you unwise;
For all that you are is to be all that you can
For you are the dream, you are my man.

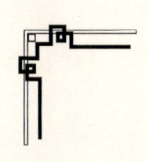

How Could I Tell

I walk no more on soft green mosses,
Under the tree where green branch tosses;
Where scent of leaf and red rose swinging,
Perfumes the wind with soft scent clinging.

I walk no more by the ocean dreaming,
Where sunbeams fly with grey gulls screaming;
Over the cliffs where wild waves falling,
Sweep up the sound with echoes calling.

I hear no more the sea shells story,
Along the shore with sunset's glory;
Only the song from the dark cave's hollow,
That siren song I dare not follow.

Words you spoke left me broken hearted,
For now I find you have departed.
I loved you well but you left me lonely,
How could I tell if you loved me only?

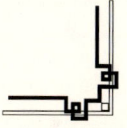

The Pyramid

Immovable forever in the shifting sand,
The ancient pyramids of Egypt stand;
Where chariots of Pharaoh once flew by,
Wearing their armor ready to die.

A monument you stand to hold the dead,
The body you hold sleeps in a silent bed;
You stand a mute witness to history,
And the story you tell is a mystery.

Built with the blood of other men's sorrow,
Your time today is an endless tomorrow.
You have seen the chariots passing by,
You've touched the eagles as they fly.

The splendor of your ancient stones,
Bear silent witness as you prevail alone;
You stand in the sun, a shrine for all to see,
Touching the skies of eternity.

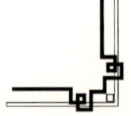

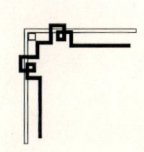

Rachel's Tears

Close now the starry curtains of the night
Lest the dream fade for a child who could not stay;
As wings stretch out to embrace the night
And take her where night meets day.

The silence from former broken years
Torn by a sob and whispered prayer;
Is filled with anguish that won't console fears
In days to come where no comfort lingers there.

There comes a voice from echoes of the past,
A sigh from Rama weeping her sad lot;
Lamentation for a woman's cry is cast
As Rachel grieves her babes that were not.

There's no comfort in a cold grey tomb
Where time has found its relentless grasp;
A child so early from the womb
Finds comfort in death's tender clasp.

Matthew 2:18-A voice was heard in Rama, lamentation, weeping and great mourning. Rachel weeping for her children,
refusing to be comforted because they are no more.

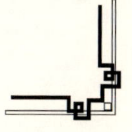

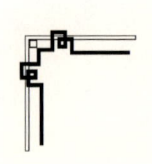

Froggie Dreams

There once was a frog that sat on a log,
And the home he chose was in a marsh bog.
He sat on the log with a great big smile,
And watched flies buzz in the sun awhile.

The clothes he wore were a bright green,
The colour was like a green string bean.
There on his back were occasional spots,
That decorated his coat with gay polka dots.

Now frog can't sit still without eating,
And the flies flying by were so fleeting;
But frog had a tongue that was very quick,
He used it with abandon, just like a joy stick.

Sitting in the sun he watched the flies,
And snatched them up to their surprise.
There were many who came but many were gone,
And those that came didn't stay very long.

The eating was great but he gained weight,
Which to his alarm; caused him to inflate.
For his clothes no longer seemed to fit,
Which gave him the urge to no longer sit.

So he decided to lose weight, to go on a diet,
To croak sad songs and not to be quiet;
For forcing himself not to eat it seems,
Take joy out of green froggie dreams.

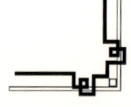

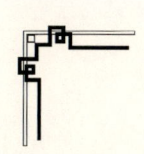

Forgiveness

If by my grave you someday pass,
And see a stone with my name;
Spend time with me, sit in the grass,
And pray you can forgive my shame.

If I didn't pass all that was true,
Or fell beneath your portion of desire;
If I didn't do all that was right,
My heart lives in fear of its own empty fire.

Then let your sorrow drown its tear
On your cheek in sadness fall;
Forget my failure, keep my memory near,
For what I was to you over all.
And if you can't reach out and bless,
Give me compassion in forgiveness.

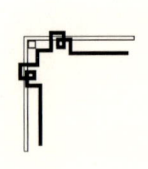

Over the Edge

These men whose empty eyes are bright
As vacant windows set in stone;
Sift through the echoes of black night
When fog and wind speak silence alone.

On forsaken paths and in empty halls
One can see them deformed and hollow;
Like wild shapes that climb prison walls
They hold the vision they could not follow.

Open the door softly, the faceless form
Weaves strands of life into a dream;
When the sun shines through his storm
Little men journey through what had been.

An old bent man whispers to the door
With the smell of death from the grave;
To lift the silence and hear the roar
Of voices of those they could not save.

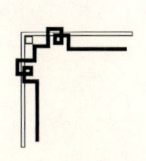

Clouds

Clouds of lace fly high in the sky,
They ride the wind and rest in the blue;
Their billowing white should not deny,
A rite of passage going through.

Sullen clouds are bringing rain,
They whisper secrets left unsaid;
The drink they bring is sweet champagne,
To kiss the flowers that bloom in their bed.

Clouds catch wings of restless bird,
To fly with wind and whisper a song;
They carry to all where it's not been heard,
With breath of neither right nor wrong.

Wind that comes blows puffs of white,
It takes the clouds then leaves them alone;
Then all that's left is scattered light,
For clouds that were are now gone home.

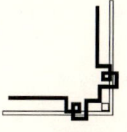

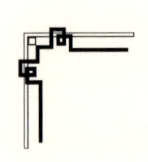

The Lark

From darkest night to early dawn,
The guns sound loud with no abate;
The feeble sun is looking on,
Blood splattered fields of hate.
As if despised to rise again,
A sudden sound from the dark;
From the fields of waving grain,
The spiraling sound of a lark.

A sweet torrent of melody,
That showers from the sky;
A new fleet winged enemy,
That can't be hushed though we try.
There she flew on joyful wings;
With outspread feathers of fleece,
Tossing hopes of such strange things,
As pleasure, joy and peace.

Singer of songs, you must know,
That we on earth make hell;
Or is it that your song must show,
That perhaps all is well?
Fearless wings fly not in vain,
For they soar in a sky so blue;
And we who love war's red stain,
Lift eyes to see heaven too!

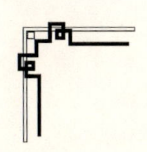

The Renegade

A renegade came in on his horse from the west
With spurs on his boots and a fringe on his vest;
The tilt of his hat was folly's own heat
And his carved boots were full of big feet;
His engraved leather belt held pistols and things
And an old deck of cards held aces and kings.

Lovely Juliette sat there feeling remorse
When the dude came in riding a black horse;
Her loveliness gave him a pectoral glow
And he reigned in his horse with a powerful "Whoa";
Then he turned to the woman with an ecstatic smile
And boldly asked if he could stay awhile.

With flustered mind she blinked eyes in fright
But Juliette smiled and said that he might;
So in through the entrance rode the mysterious dude
With a proud mind and feeling a bit lewd;
He strode up to the landlord and cleaned out the bar
And the landlord threatened to coat him with tar;
The judge banged his gavel and charged him for same
Then the renegade left and rode off with his dame.

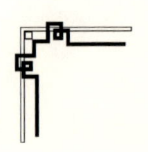

Memories

A lily in the pond
A mountain beyond;
A blue sky in spring
A bird on the wing.
The rippling call
Of a waterfall;
A soft spring rain
A robin's refrain.
Fields full of flowers
Spending long hours
With arms around you
Speak words not a few.
Such little things
To remember for years;
The songs we sing
Memories with tears.

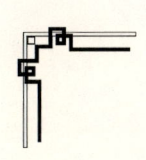

Under September Skies

One night all alone in the garden
Under September skies;
The moon was gone but the starlight shone
And glowed like your beautiful eyes.
Away from the shimmer and lamplight
I stood so lonely there;
While the joy of the throng was loud in song
And floated on the air.

You looked down through the starlight
And I looked up at you;
A memory came that I could not name
A feeling unknown and new.
We were lovers for a short time only
So why should I feel such pain?
To know you would go where tomorrow
Would not bring you to me again.

The time that flies fast between us
Can never be captured I know;
For hours now sleep and eyes now weep
As the turmoil spins below.
But I know that I shall remember
Though I will try my best to forget;
How I looked in your eyes under September skies
After the moon had set.

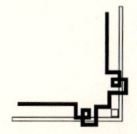

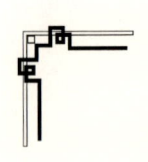

Invite a Kiss

Rosy cheeks and sweet round hips,
Invite a kiss from parted lips.
I need to hold your supple form,
To feel your pulse, to keep me warm.

In my mind the thoughts allure,
The thinking that has no cure;
To probe the secrets of my will,
And hold the dream that keeps me still.

Let's while away the dusk of night,
That brings the morning rays of light;
To find some happy dreams of pleasure,
And share the time with all we treasure.

Stay right here, rest at my side,
And share the hopes that I can't hide;
Speak soft words that can be known,
And never leave my thoughts alone.

Let's try to find and trace a thought,
And bring to light all we've sought;
For joy that binds your soul and mine,
Will keep us close till the end of time.

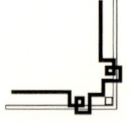

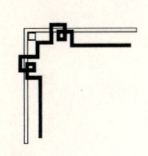

When I Meet You

Wind blows branches
Crimson leaves fall;
Soft shadows dance
On the sunlit wall.

The wind softly whispers
Secrets to the trees;
Then I'm reminded
Of much more than these.

In the soft twilight
When ever I meet you;
The trees are more crimson
And the sky is more blue.

When the wind calls her song
In forgotten skies;
Would it be wrong
If we were not wise?

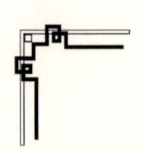

Tender Moments

All of the tender moments we shared,
When you held my hand and told me you cared;
Bring to each day a new fascination,
With lips to kiss, a heart filled with elation.
Come lie with me in fields of sweet clover,
Where honey bees fly and the scent hovers over;
Where all we feel is always new,
And minutes are plenty but the hours are few.
Let me hold you close and look in your eyes,
And speak all the words my heart denies;
For when I hold you near I can feel my heart,
Beating each moment till we have to part.
And as we walk our ways into a setting sun,
The parting of ways will merge into one.

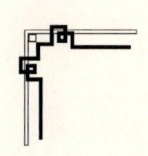

Golden Sun

The golden sun came out to play,
Lulled by the song of an empty day.
Casting a glow to light the dream,
She danced her rays upon the stream.

The depths that reach the silent tide,
Are born of hope from the prison inside;
To teach the bondsman how to praise,
The lovely warmth of sunlit days.

Perhaps the sun will wrap your soul,
With arms of light to make you whole;
Perhaps the sun will touch your face,
And fold you in her warm embrace.

Dance the path of silent sound,
And heal the wound that can't be found;
For the sun can touch and the sun can heal,
All the sorrow that seems so real.

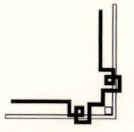

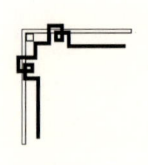

Chasing the Mouse

There was a mouse who liked to roam,
Because he didn't have a home;
But he checked around and found one nice,
That had all the comforts needed to suffice.

Now the man of the house didn't like mice,
He agreed with the thought they weren't very nice;
So he went to town and bought a gun,
And brought it home to have some fun.

The man of the house had a cat named Kitty,
She had spots and wasn't too pretty;
So Kitty saw the mouse and tried to pounce,
But the mouse saw Kitty and tried to bounce.

Now the mouse was starved but found some cheese,
But the cheese he found made him sneeze;
The sneeze was so loud the man came running,
But the mouse went to hide because he was cunning.

The man ran with his gun right through the door,
While the mouse kept running around the floor.
He cocked his gun and shot at the mouse,
And the smoke from the gun filled the whole house.

But the mouse kept running filled with surprise,
Because all the man hit were blue bottle flies.
And Kitty the cat was scared out of her wits,
She went down to the basement and threw some fits.

Now the man was upset and not having fun,
So he called the poor mouse a son of a gun;
But the mouse was glad with no reason to be sad,
For the man with the gun was really mad.

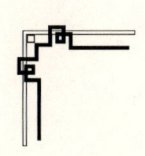

That Place

That place between sleep and waking
A time when you remember your dreams;
Sometimes the vision clears only
When our eyes are washed with tears.
There are times when a heart is aching
For love is not all that it seems;
Sometimes it gifts you with feeling lonely
And leaves a heart close to breaking.

So many in life are there to hurt you
Can we know if they are worth the pain
O do we allow the fetters and chain?
There's so much to say when I look in your eyes
There's so much to feel when the spirit dies;
Each day I love you more but you'll never know
There's so much in my heart I can't show.
I'd hold you forever if you'd only let me
But I know dear, you will forget me;
So I dream of us together and how it could be
For all you are will stay a secret part of me.

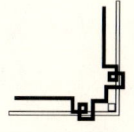

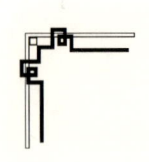

The Battle

The menace of war with the chaos of life,
The peril of ocean when tempests are rife;
The danger of jungle where feral beasts hide,
The terror that lies in a mountain slide.
Yet all these are simple child's play,
Or frivolous sport on a summer's day;
With sad battles that rouse and vex,
The heart and soul of love and sex.

Struggle and hardship and beast of prey,
Are there to menace human clay:
The bird uncaged can take to wing,
But the hazard of love is another thing;
Once under the torment of passion's control,
Love crushes the body and steals the soul.
A minute of rapture, an age of despair,
These are the gifts of love's warfare.

Always and forever since time began,
When man dared woman and woman lured man;
In that sweet peril that prowls and lies,
A bloodless conflict when eyes meet eyes.
That careless menace, forever sweet,
Whose forlorn end is joy's defeat;
Now and forever till time has passed,
On passion's altar hearts shall come last.

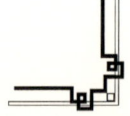

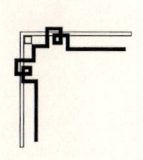

I Love Him So

Like the bend of the larch in the wind of dawn,
Like a twilight sky or a starlit lawn;
Like fleecy clouds in their shifting white,
As capricious as the moon is bright
Is the soul of him.

Like whispering leaves when the woods are green,
Sing with a brook through a night time dream;
With sweet mysteries that his eyes withhold,
Passion to me he never has told
To the soul of me.

Like the vision of midnight that follows my eye,
The shadow he casts that will not reply
To the song in my heart; for all that I know
It brings me to the place where I want to go
For I love him so.

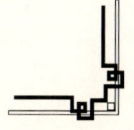

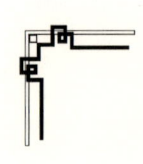

Be Not Afraid

The mountains and hills shake at His tread,
The resurrection is nigh He calls to the dead;
The moon in the heavens grows pale at His wrath,
The sun of the morn disappears from its path.
God of the universe, maker of all,
We ask for your mercy, at your feet we do fall.

The earth's stealthy riches are exposed to your sight,
Nor veiled from you are man's deeds of the night;
The beasts grow timid as they bow at your feet,
And the winds of the sea at your command retreat.
Forever your greatness over all things,
Maker of all, our King of kings.

When the mountains erupt their flames to the sky,
And lightning's forked tongue shouts back in reply;
When the stars in the heaven died in their place,
And malevolent man laughed in your face;
With infinite mercy your anger grew still,
Our crucified Lord on Golgotha's hill.

Yet you forgive all dear Father above,
And we owe all for your infinite love;
The hands pierced with nails you give for our aid,
You speak through your word to not be afraid.
You are able to comfort whenever we call,
For you there is nothing too great or too small.
Always you hear when we kneel down to pray,
Precious Redeemer helps us find our way

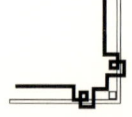

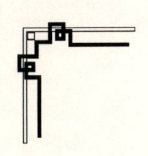

Windows

I looked thru my window and happened to see,
All the world passing round me;
There were white picket fences,
And people sitting on painted park benches.
Children laughing and flying a kite,
With a tail swirling in the sunlight;
A white wooden trellis with buckets of roses;
To scent the air and tickle pink noses.
A bird perched in a tree chirping her song,
Over a nest where her babies belong;
And around the corner came a sweet gentle breeze,
Tossing the tassels of yellow larch trees.
And shadows that linger to paint the lawn,
Touched fingers of light to tint the dawn;
And all the while the hours flew by.
Delighting my soul and painting my eye.

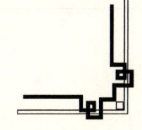

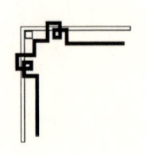

Bite of the Flea

You never loved an apple tree,
As much as I hate a flea;
They leap, they spring without wings,
And march to tunes that mother sings.

They hide in rugs and in stuffed chairs,
And pay no heed to anxious stares;
They infest dogs and prey on cats,
And hide in woven straw doormats.

Fleas that went to an idiot's school,
Have no time to play the fool;
But mother is a saint at war,
With all the fleas that feast on gore.

When mother takes out spray for fleas,
They see her coming on her knees;
They hide in cracks and nether parts,
Waiting till the fume departs.

Let us now make a firm vow,
Those fleas are bringing trouble now;
So mother sprayed the house with gas,
And all the fleas breathed their last.

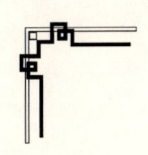

Ocean's Lullaby

There are none of love's daughters
That are as lovely as thee;
Like the ripple of still waters
Is your sweet music to me.
Then the murmur was causing
The wild ocean's mad pausing;
And the waves lay still gleaming
While the ebb tide rose dreaming.

The moonshine is weaving
Bright silver beams on the deep;
With the waves gently heaving
The grey gulls fast asleep.
So the stars shine before you
The wind sighs to adore you;
With a song so full of emotion
Like the surge of the ocean.

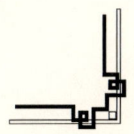

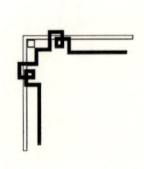

Samson and Delilah

Yesterday with its yearnings and sorrow
With its shadows and sunbeams at length;
Have gone where the fears of tomorrow
Took a man whose conceit was his strength.

His transient raptures brought shame
From the temptress who ravished his soul;
Taking strength and tarnished his name
From the power he had that she stole.

Sleep on in the arms that still hold you
Let your eyes not shed all their tears;
For the hand that caressed has now sold you
To the sad treachery of defiant shears.

The Philistine put out his eyes
He was bound in fetters and chains;
The darkness that brought him captivity
Took the blood that flowed in his veins.

For the ransom of a corrupt Aphrodite
Whose strength was extinguished by desire;
The pillars are destroyed by the mighty
While his glory has perished in fire.

Men That March

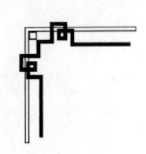

Men that march through crooked streets,
And highways paved with stone;
Men that killed with bayonets,
Some never more came home.

There are those who pay the piper,
Some pay to call the tune;
And those who came a marching,
Sweat in sunshine's noon.

The men are marching all in step,
When still of evening comes;
And yet the beat of marching feet,
Step time with muffled drums.

To partner with the dance of death,
Needs choose their partner well;
For dancing to that lonely tune,
Is a sorry way to hell.

War is such a random fight,
We are kin in all but name;
And all who died in foreign lands,
Never knew their blood's the same.

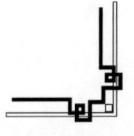

Sonnet

The flowers in my garden grow,
With fields of gold around;
And in the wood blue violets blow,
Where daffodils are found.
Sweet smells the earth so wet with rain,
While roses scent with bloom;
Through the field and winding lane,
Breathes the song of spring's perfume.
Though field and wood about me lie,
Silent in soft delight;
I hear the moonbeam's tender sigh,
In the silence of the night.
Yet such a short while ago,
I recalled the memory of winter's snow.

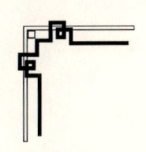

Songbird

Dear little songbird,
With your beak of gold;
Wearing untidy feathers,
Sing a song sweetly told.
The wings of my songbird,
Seek blue fields above;
Where my feathered songster,
Serenades his love.
With wings opened wide,
He soars in the skies;
His darting and swooping,
Give delight to my eyes.
He sings in the twilight,
Where my soul comes to be;
Joining the fireflies,
High up in the tree.
Dear little songbird,
Sing your hymn in the blue;
For I have no wings,
To fly with you.

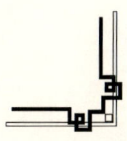

A Wild Sweet Night

A wild sweet night I would spend with you,
With arms open wide I would blend with you;
To wander with the wind in Elysian fields,
Where poppies sleep and your touch heals.

Let's sip the dew of midnight's wine,
Turn back the clock, lose track of time.
My body yearns and I yield to you,
With a heart that burns I turn to you.

The promise of Eden is forever there,
And the promise of love is ours to share;
Let's join hands and dance with the night,
As hearts join as one to romance in our flight.

Let the magic of fingers join with mine,
Let me look in your eyes, the feast is fine;
Till the rose of morning brings dawn's early ray,
And the loving of night greets the reality of day.

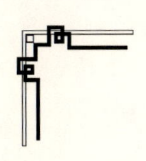

October

Quench the sun with a clinging mist
And adorn the land with amethyst;
The grape already touched with frost
Finds clustered fruit will soon be lost.
The wind catches the leaves that fall
And birds head south with anxious call;
Frost comes quick to lick the flowers
Who droop their heads in long lost hours.
The crimson leaves brush bark that's rough
To show leaves and bark are tree enough;
And in the woods squirrels gather nuts
While sleepy beasts look for winter huts;
And the tremulous wing of a butterfly
Etch fluttering flight in a sapphire sky.
Up above shines a full harvest moon
To hide the memories of long lost June;
She shines with the aura of a gypsy rose
With the in between of winter's snows.
Then the faded earth and leaden sky
Bid October a sad goodbye.

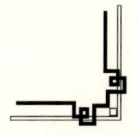

Spring Is Here

Spring's shy eyes are waking,
Not quite open yet;
Her busy fingers making,
Green grass and violet.
Dreary winter is now over,
Bluebirds sing by the lane,
There I see my lover,
Spring's here again.

The days now grow longer,
Than the day we had before;
The fragrance there is stronger,
With flowers seen once more.
The woodland trees are shady,
In the softly falling rain;
Come kiss your lady,
It's springtime again.

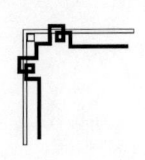

Inspiration

Tell me of hope for the world is sad enough
Without my complaint to make it more rough;
Find new faces to give the heart cheer
And hold close all those who are most dear;
For earth knows the perpetual drain
Of persistent sorrow and unceasing pain.

Tell me of faith, for the world's better without
Your dreams of folly and melancholy doubt;
If you trust in God and not in yourself
And will be able to put your doubts on a shelf
To give peace of mind so faith can come
Then no one will mind if your mouth is dumb.

Let's speak of health, this sad endless tale
Of human troubles that are boring and stale.
You cannot win or profit or please
By harping on the dischord of stubborn disease;
Say you feel fine, the world is good to you
And before you know, it will all come true.

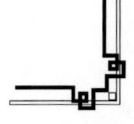

I Will Not Wake You

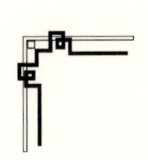

I will not wake you with tears I cry,
To warm the bed where you lie;
The silence of your nights alone,
Never hears the winds that moan.

Never to touch my lips or eyes,
With your mouth or tender sighs;
Your weary clay has turned to dust,
My lonely way has lost its trust.

I have washed you with my tears,
Remembering I held you all those years;
But I miss your pillow and your place,
I miss the nearness of your face.

I bring a flower for your stone,
To grace a memory I bear alone;
Times spent in happier years,
Are joined with joys and silent tears.

Make place for me ere I weep,
And wake you from your rest and sleep;
Make room for me to cry with you,
Hold me for I would die with you.
Let's capture all we used to be,
And find it all in eternity.

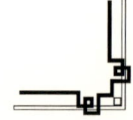

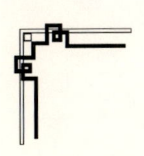

Forbidden

Down a crooked Arab street,
A grey eyed soldier strode;
And shrouded to her feet,
She stepped from her abode.

Now luck may shield a favored wife,
Who leaves the harem hive;
But emptiness is in her heart,
When she is one of five.

If black eyes shine with secret fire,
And meet the yearning eyes of grey;
The ancient story of desire,
Will surely have its way.

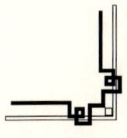

A Journey

As we travel along with a heart full of song,
We've a dream that hangs on a rope;
Like a lantern of light, shining at night,
She shines on the fair abode called hope.

The arms of time roll round as we climb,
And our youth fades fast with the years;
With a soul grown numb, with sorrows we come,
Back to the valley of tears.

Still forward we press with faults to confess,
With hearts that need much repair;
Where glistening gleams on soft sunbeams,
Shining on a world of despair.

All lives need change but the heart can estrange,
A soul from the Father above;
And reviling the rod administered by God,
Brings chastening He calls Love.

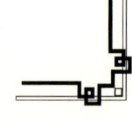

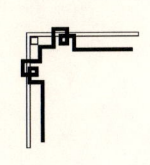

In Between

Today is nearly over,
And tomorrow's not quite here;
There's a glow of a silver lining
As twilight drifts so near.

This time is in between
The precious here and now;
A whisper of a moment
That captures then and how.

Today is fraught with trouble
Tomorrow is but a dream;
I need to know my heart
To find what's in between.

I opened up my eyes
To see all that might be;
And I awakened to the wonder
That sets a spirit free.

Today is almost over
Then tomorrow will be today;
Time will slowly stretch her arms
And steal the hours away.

At last the hour is turning
Today has gone somewhere;
Now that it is over
Tomorrow is everywhere.

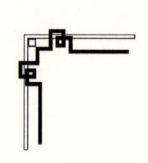

When He Came

I waited for him as the soldier comes
With a beating of drums and trumpet call;
But he arrived instead with a quiet tread
That my ears never heard at all.

I though he would come like the blazing sun
And claim me for his bride;
But in the soft twilight of a starlit night
He stood there at my side.

I thought he would come as loud thunder
That shouts to the midnight skies;
Instead he came as a whisper
And the finger of love touched my eyes.

I dreamed of the fire that shone in his eye
Might give mine a more tender glow;
But I saw in his face a more intimate grace
That I discovered not long ago.

I thought he would come in the tumult
Of ten thousand voices in song;
Instead he came in soft silence
And brought me to where I belong.

I hoped his coming would awaken my soul
As the seas are split by storm's strife;
But he brought me balm of a sublime calm
And tranquility that crowned my life.

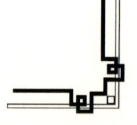

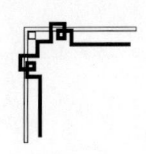

Time to Go

I know the bitter sorrow and pain
For one sided love is a deathly woe;
It is kind compared to that time I know
When love's passion is on the wane.

When I feel the ache and know the grace
That gave glory to my night and day;
Is now dying with sorrows of grey
Becoming dull and so commonplace.
When my whispers of love fall on deaf ears,
And my hand reaches yours without thrill;
When we cannot compel by force or will
The sweet passions that had no tears;
When the dream has gone and love is asleep
When you no longer want to be near;
And all I cherish has gone from our year
Then it is the sad time to weep.

But there are no tears left to heal the woe
For I will see you with sad dry eyes;
If we try to hold it the faster love flies
And I will know it is time to go.

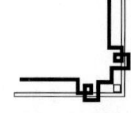

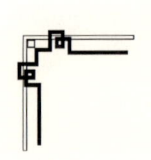

September

Autumn's laden with fruit and ripening grains,
To be harvested after the latter day rains.
Wild geese fly waving their wings goodbye,
In patterns like arrows in a faraway sky.

The vesper bell that rings in the song,
Tolls for a summer that stayed too long;
Now the Master is painting all the green trees,
With scarlet, gold and russet brown leaves.

The passions of heat from a summer's sun,
Shine more gently now that summer is done;
Now is the time to put the treasures to sleep,
To cover the gardens, the pathways to sweep.

The hazel nut trees in the still mossy bower,
Shelters with care autumns last lonely flower;
And the soft sunny days of golden September,
Carry us through to the cold of December.

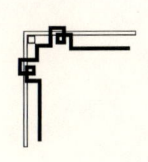

I Walk Alone

In worlds where peace is never known,
I live to wait and walk alone;
To listen as the lark sings her song,
A melody that lasts all day long.
The sounds of joy that fill the wood,
Voiced not to silence if I could;
Where shafts of golden sunlight burn,
To burnish each green branch and fern.

The earth is wet with summer rain,
Splashing drops on wood and lane;
Where woodland voices wrap me round,
Where peace and love are always found.
Where all the meadow lilies grow,
Bending in the winds that blow;
Where clumps of violets rest in sleep,
There branches of the willows weep.

Where wings of clouds hover over,
To cover fields of sweet clover;
And see bluebells touch the skies,
With rabbits sitting looking wise.
I hear the wind call my name,
The song she sang is never the same.
I do not ask for things unknown,
But to touch and see and walk alone.

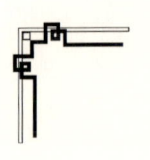

Pearl of Great Price

I hired a ship to take a trip,
Over stormy ocean;
I shielded my eye from a stormy sky,
And the boat's constant motion.

There was a diving suit, a map to read,
And travels we had to sail;
So we left the shore as we leaned on the oar,
And held on to the rail.

The trip was long the sea was rough,
Our destiny was fate;
Day was drear as the place drew near,
For the hour was growing late.

The sky grew dark and wind came up,
To catch the fragile sail;
So we held on tight as the coming night,
Brought darkness to prevail.

We lowered the sail, prepared to stop,
So we could rest in sleep;
But the boat would rock, the wind would mock,
Waves that plied the deep.

We never slept but always kept,
Our hopes the boat would hold;
We fought the storm till the rays of morn,
Brought calm to waters cold.

Morning light bade goodbye to night,
And day dawned bright and clear,
So we sailed along to a sailor's song,
As providence drew near.

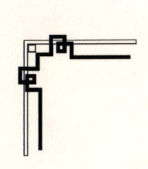

At last we came to the place we claim,
That tattered sail unfurls;
We prepared to strive for a cold deep dive,
To look for precious pearls.

We were set to dive in waters dark,
Down to the oyster bed;
Where fishes float and grey sharks gloat,
And hearts are filled with dread.

We filled the net and strived to set,
A time to heed the call,
And shells we reaped were gently heaped,
In a net to carry all.

After many dives we came up alive,
And dumped our shells with pleasure.
Anxious to see if adversity,
Would give a royal treasure.

I picked a shell that was one of the last,
And opened it with haste;
It was covered with moss and seemed a loss,
But the pearl I saw was chaste.

I gazed with surprise not trusting my eyes,
At something I'd never seen;
It glowed like a light, like a star in the night,
Infused with moonlit sheen.

Its splendor was lovely, perfect and round,
No fault was there to see;
This was the pearl of great price I found,
Sought in epiphany.

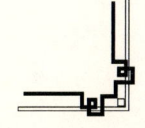

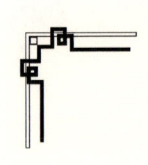

Reason to Be

I am, I was and will be
As I live in each heart through death;
I yield to no oath or no shackle
I stimulate all with my breath.

I speak the words of love's passion
I know the damage of sorrow;
I hold the reigns of compassion
I reach for the dreams of tomorrow.

I dream in the fire of the jewel
I taste the blood of the tree;
I speak to the beast of the forest
I walk this earth and am free.

I've felt the sharp arrows of pain
I've joined in the laughter of mirth;
I've danced to the devil's refrain
And know life is not better than birth.

I don't live in a convent or cave,
Or an ancient kingdom above;
Here on this side of the grave
Is where I shall labor and love.

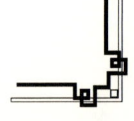

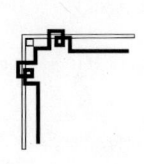

Up In the Willow

Up in the willow climbing I go,
With the sky above and the earth below;
Each branch a step up to the sky,
Each step taken where feathered wings fly.

Up in the willow I see all around,
And all I am seeing is leafy green ground;
With lily and primrose to tint the hill,
Saying good bye to winter's chill.

Up in the willow I hear rippling streams,
Carrying waters of opaline dreams;
And the persistent call of a waterfall,
Echoes throughout a green willow hall.

Up in the willow I feel the wind,
Rocking, and shocking brown etched limb;
And trees with leaves licked with gold,
Float down to earth with stories untold.

Up in the willow I see all ablaze,
Scarlet sumac painting fall's sunny days;
While looking over earth's bright sunny scapes,
With fields of hay and purple vine grapes.

The wind is flying in its lonely quest,
From north to south and east to west;
Singing the lyrics of September's song,
In lithe willow branches all day long.

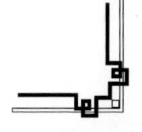

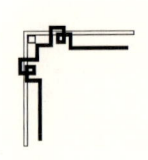

Buds of May

The hope that brings the buds of May,
Brings a glow to light the way;
For winter came and now it's past.
Taking with it the stormy blast.

We are waiting for the buds of May,
To bring the scent that wants to stay;
Sitting with secrets in the sun,
Waiting to open when cold is done.

Now we know that the buds of May,
Bring hope and dreams that drift away;
Shall the wind be called to tease,
The buds that hide in orchard trees?

At last the darling buds of May,
Shed their green and drift away;
While blossoms blooming in the sun,
Bring visions to see for everyone.

The buds of May are too soon gone,
Their time with us was not to long;
They bade goodbye one afternoon,
And the buds of May burst into bloom.

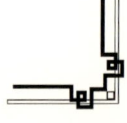

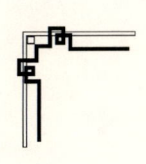

Phantoms

Phantoms of all my lovely sins,
Who come to me at night;
Bring sad fingers of the rain,
To wash my dreams from sight.

Phantoms turn your eyes and ears,
Give no more thought for sorrow;
For you have spent my future years,
In surviving for tomorrow.

My tears are falling with the rain,
Capricious and unholy;
Tapping at the window pane,
Running forlorn and slowly.

I have lived with all the beauty,
Of the churchyard's friendless flowers;
Let me this night find duty
In mystic moonlit bowers.

Every withered leaf shall fade,
When bright October passes;
And yet the day brings sun and shade
To sift through fragile grasses.

Phantoms of temptations heed,
My plea to be forgiving;
Don't you know that I have need,
To be dying with the living?

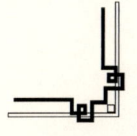

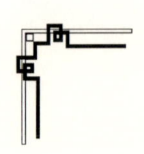

Snowdrops

You blossom too soon dear snowdrops of March
Secluded in the cold dark earth;
The snowflakes of winter still haunt the sky
Weary with sorrow to greet your birth.
One warm day you awakened from sleep
And sang with the wind's soft breath;
It caressed your eyes with the lips of spring
But you awakened to winter and the arms of death.

Where is the promise she pledged to you
The passion of sun and whisper of the breeze;
The hyacinth's heavy scent and purple bloom
And the robin's song high up in the trees?

Birds are yet hushed and the branch is yet bare
The snowflakes fall on the crest of the hill;
And your sodden petals lie pressed to the ground
With the winds of winter's grim chill.
The snowflakes conceal the spot where you lie
Not finding space in a winter's noon;
They are covered with white so no one will know
The grave of the snowdrops that flowered too soon.

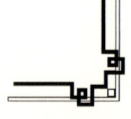

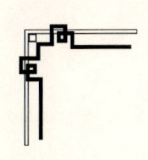

Hope for Dreams

Blossoms of hope and hope for dreams,
Shed hope for trust of silly schemes;
When all the world is spinning around,
And trust and hope are lost not found.

As we strolled through the meadow rue,
When all was false and nothing new;
You turned your timid eye to gaze,
On trust and hope through misty haze.

Yet we are shadows that haste away,
Souls that know not how to play;
For our body is gone but the spirit is not,
And the sorrow is we've never been taught.

In the street where dreams drift by,
Where children dance and mothers cry;
When silence rests so cold and deep,
To chasten death and lull to sleep.

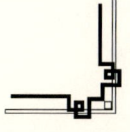

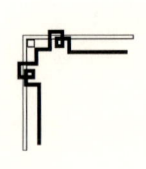

Songbird in My Garden

I am delighted by your choice,
Dear wee songbird with your voice;
Now when I look up in your tree,
A fuzzy head looks down at me.

Beady eyes, bright yellow crown,
Sits as I look up and you look down;
Stretch your tiny feathered wing,
And open wide your beak to sing.

The dappled lawn and coloured flowers,
I'll call them yours instead of ours;
No prowling cat will I tolerate,
Your little nest will be inviolate.

Your airborne flight, your yellow coat,
Sing silver songs from your throat,
Bring joy to me my songbird true,
Come to my garden where I'll live with you.

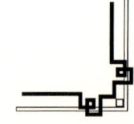

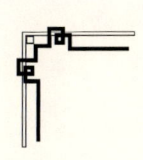

Eternity of Tears

The fields are full of daisies
The skies are sapphire blue;
By the arbor in the garden
I wait, my love for you.
The garden blooms with poppies
Their flame burns bright and gay;
With scent of rose and honey
Will you come to me today?

Through the hours together
In scented copse we lie;
In the blaze of golden weather
Beneath a deep blue sky.
When we would have our pleasure
For such a transitory stay;
Should we squander leisure
Will you come to me today?

Life hasn't much to offer
Man has naught to lose;
This day chance will proffer
What we dare not now refuse.
We will take this fleeting hour
In the silent hazy gloom;
While the poppies are in flower
And the roses are in bloom

If time remembers later
And tries to claim her due;
Our grieving will be greater
Than the wonder I had with you.
When ignited by your laughter
Through sad and lonely years
I will find in the hereafter
An eternity of tears.

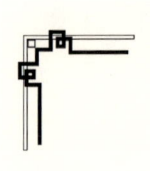

Evening Dew

When twilight's spectral fingers fold
Sweet blossoms of each hue;
Some half opened bud will hold
Its pearls of evening dew.

Touched with every sunshine hour
The eternal earth has shown;
All the perfume of the flower
Till it finally becomes its own.

We that wait may never find
A chance to sing our praise;
For memories we seek to bind
Take the scent of fading days.

The poet who has never spent
His words in futile strain;
For him the misty dewdrops lent
Their diamonds to the rain.

Unfastened in their fragrant bell
They tell their own dear tales;
Then from the cloud from which they fell
Their haunting scent exhales.

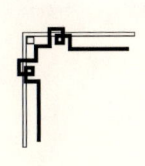

Conscience

When I look through the curtain
I see humanity's plight;
Our lives seem so uncertain
There's little that is alright.
Yet out of confusion I come groping
To see a world dressed in bloom;
With my heart created for hoping
I find no comfort in gloom.

We see from boundary to border
That humanity wars with each race;
With rebellion and irate disorder
We exist in a shameful place.
But I think as the sun is setting
I could embrace peace without strife;
For my mind needs a way of forgetting
All except the beauty of life.

I knew from childhood's beginning
We live in a season of woe;
With suffering, sadness and sinning
For my conscience told me so.
The truth of it all is so tragic
I wept for all that was wrong;
Then by the art of sweet magic
My heart found a new song.

The years keep coming and going
A jumble of pleasure and pain;
But the sadness I feel is showing
That evil is on the gain.
My heart should now be grieving
For I find there is no comforting;
But I always keep believing
Life is a miraculous thing.

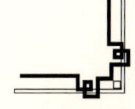

Elements

See the spreading beauty
In the blush of June;
Yahweh is creator
With who we must commune.
Do you hear the wind blowing?
That is Yahweh's breath;
When time is always going
To the arms of death.
Do you see the ocean streaming?
That is Yahweh's blood;
Like the rose that's dreaming
From the new burst bud.
His face that there is shining
With wisdom in His eyes;
Is there for our complying
As the need arise.
Fire, air and moving water
With the moist and verdant sod;
Are elements changing ever
Of a never changing God.
When your dream on wings ascends
Where dreams are always free;
Then the face of God descends
And brings eternity.

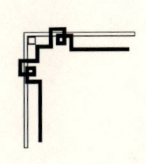

Licketty Split

Time is flying, no need to sit,
Get up and at it, licketty split.
A new day has come, it's time to get going;
There's no time now to be easygoing.

There are places to go and things to do,
Hours to spend with a new point of view;
There are gardens to rake and lawns to mow,
Dishes to wash and clothes to sew.

Time to clean house, to put on a shine,
To take the pickles out of the brine;
Time to sit and talk on the phone,
To go for a walk with my thought all alone.

It's been a great day with no time to rest,
I've raced through the day and given my best.
Now that I've gotten this out of my head,
It's time to lie down and go to bed.

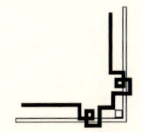

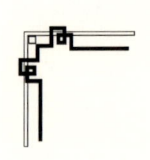

Lives to Live

I need more lives for me to live
In this universe of beauty;
I plan more days to find new ways
Of doing freedom's duty.
I need not more joy than this
For I am life's dear lover;
And when I wage to turn the page
I'd never want another.

The glorious pledge of sunny Spring
With sweet June coming after;
Bring autumn sighs and summer's cries
Lost in winter's laughter.
With a virgin moon and scorching noon
And stars in a thousand nights;
I'd need no heaven if love be given
With all its sweet delights.

There are many splendors for the eye
And such music for the ear;
The mind would reel with all to feel
And see to touch and hear.
There's many ways to spend the days
And more to do what's kind;
For bread now cast on waters past
Returns again I find.

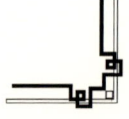

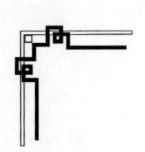

There are such gifted souls to know
And so much more to learn;
While a promise rests in earth's warm breast
And unknown stars still burn.
In six days God made all the earth
The bible is known to say;
Six lives I need to plant a seed
Of love, with one for each dear day.

But sad if love should walk away
Or hide his face from me;
Six lives aren't much if I had such
But one's all that need be.
With unhappy May and sorry June
Cold dawns and weary night;
A sorry world through space was hurled
When love had lost her light.

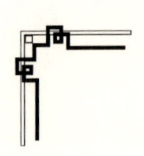

Till You Came

I was so safe until you came,
But you look with gentle eyes;
Your smile lights my night,
And puts stars in all my skies.

Tis the time, it is the season,
That captures many a heart;
For love needs not a reason,
To keep two souls apart.

It's the walk we take in sunshine,
Time spent in summer's rain;
To hear the birdsong calling,
That takes away the pain.

To share the twilight hours,
When the moon is hanging low;
Midst all the scented flowers,
Is too sweet to let it go.

I found someone so special,
When summer's days were long;
When trees were white with blossoms,
And birds were light with song.

But endless fears lie in wait,
What if they leave me desolate?
If you were lost what would I do?
If death should fall in love with you?

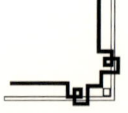

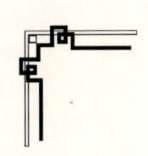

Vanity

The great creation sighs
And suns wax and wane;
Fate concedes or denies
With loss or gain.
We endure the praise and blame;
The folly of insanities
With grandeur and shame
With comfort in vanities.

We search the sea for pearls
Or find them in a drain;
We dress our head with curls
Or put up with the pain.
We're humble or we reign
We wonder or we brawl;
We hunt for pride and fame
But nothing comes at all.

Life's a vapor that curls
From what's left of the flame;
The wind whips and whirls
The fragment frail and vain
Where everything's insane.
What's left for king or thief
May transport joy or grief;
Consumed in a common flame
Are prudence or insanities;
For these things we came
To lose comfort in sad vanities.

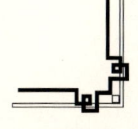

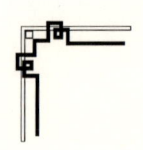

Adversity

How cautious I was while going my way,
When adversity upon me was thrust;
Words spoken in my ear to stay,
With evil thoughts to break my trust.
But you who trifle with my heart,
I once loved but now cause such grief;
For when the pain that tears apart,
Is now the soul for each reckless thief.
Now all these things need be confessed,
To bring conclusion to this affair;
To rid the soul of its forlorn unrest;
And ease the pain that lingers there.
For even if I go my way I fear,
My thwarted heart would shed a tear.

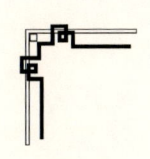

Spring Morning

We stood on tiptoe to look all around,
At all the springtime delights I found;
The clouds were white as flocks new shorn,
That gild the sky in dawn's early morn.

Enchanting sounds from bright eyed things,
That float in the sky on gauzy wings;
Singing to all the drooping flowers,
Fresh and sweet from spring time showers.

They lift their heads to shake the dew,
To give it back to the sky so blue;
So immense was the silent loneliness,
Such solitude I loved not less.

In silken air where sun shines through,
To gild with gold all things anew;
While sunshine beckons all to see,
The shadows dancing so merrily.

The wind blew fresh among the trees,
Lifting wings of honey bees;
And all the birdsongs gave my soul,
A springtime song that keeps me whole.

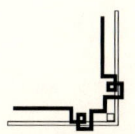

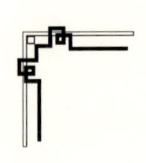

Comfort and Content

Day after day the waning of spring,
Burst into summer with blossoming;
The lark is singing wild with glee,
High on the branch of a hawthorn tree.
And daisies fair with the virgin rose,
Deck field and hedge with summer snows.
A cold white moon in a midnight sky,
Paints leaves silver as the winds pass by;
With the happy whisper of phantom feet,
Swirling like dust down the street.

The stars hang thick in the cherry tree,
The west wind scents the briny sea;
Crimson roses set heavy with dew,
Bring on the night I have captured for you.
See the dance of the swaying flowers,
As they kiss the wind in the midnight hours;
For in the night there is no ear,
Though larkspur stretch and try to hear.
Who calls this vagrant heart in me
To tread the night in odessy.

My heart is tuned to the night and sings,
For the passion I feel for all these things;
My mind is content and needs no words,
For illusions playing on minor chords:
Or torn desires and longings deep
That keep an anxious mind from sleep.
What a better gift for a life well spent,
Than the rewards of comfort and content.

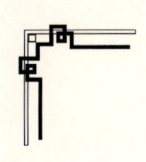

Only Make Believe

Love me though it's only make believe
Kiss me though I really know
You hold me close to just deceive;
Let that one sweet second flow
Over me lest it sink and break
My poor heart, for pity's sake.

Lend me faith for my belief
Give me from your eyes a smile;
Take away this wretched grief
And hold me close a little while.
I suffer now and surely know
You tease me with my forlorn woe.

Sing to me sweet and low
Tell me that you gently weave
Dreams of me although I know
You only play at make believe.
It hurts so much although it's plain
You are the one who scorns my pain.

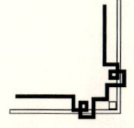

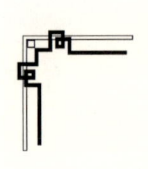

Lullaby

Sleep my baby your mother is near,
Keeping your dreams from sadness and fear;
Sunlight's asleep and bringing night,
Sleep my baby the moon shines her light.

Slumber my darling it's time to find rest,
Holding you close, your face to caress;
Sleep my baby for I'll keep you warm,
Holding you close to keep you from harm.

Rest my darling; all the world is asleep,
In my arms your dreams I will keep;
Pray that the angels will shine grace upon you,
Sleep my darling, the hours are few.

Awaken my baby for dawn's early ray,
Finds birds that sing of a bright new day;
Bringing the glow of dawn's early light,
And chasing away darkness of night.

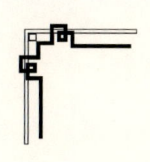

Evening Star

In the breath of summer,
The time was midnight;
With stars in their circuits,
Shining their light.
Still brighter the moon,
Midst planets like knaves;
Shines high in the sky,
Reflecting on waves.
I looked at her smile,
So remote in the sky;
Wearing her shroud,
Above clouds passing by.
And I turned to you,
My dear evening star;
More lovely you be,
Than heaven's lights are.
So shall your light shine,
As I stand and admire,
But you glow's not for me,
In your cold distant fire.

Autumn Reverie

Shifting haze, so softly trailing
Through wood and field, now veiling
Melancholy skies, holding back the tears
With wild geese flying to meet other years.
Flames of crimson torches come flinging
Leaves on knarled branches swinging;
While desolate winds come leaping
Taking flowers to their final sleeping.
In the groaning of the atmosphere
Unfolding sorrows weep with the fading year;
Fields of cluttered stubble are tangled
Rampant with weeds, dew drop spangled.
Flocks of birds leave like flying missiles
Over fields of corn and drying thistles.
Then the dream of autumn fades, paling
Through grandeur all prevailing;
When sunset fires light sky and sea
And sink in the breath of serenity.

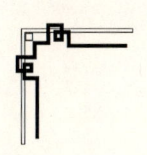

Magic

Enchantment of magic's sweet passion has bound me
With minutes and hours I now must reclaim;
Spellbound, love calls to the spirits around me
And drifts into dreams at the sound of his name.

The breath of his memory awakens from slumber;
I hear the soft whispers of a loving refrain
That stirs in my heart such an infinite hunger
With incense to scent each exquisite strain.

The face of my love comes back in a vision
With sounds of his voice in the soft grey gloom;
In a twilight of stars when the scent is Elysian
I wait for him under the plum tree in bloom.

So hushed is the flute of a love song enchanted
With music he played when his mouth was stirred;
I now hear the song so tenderly haunted
Invading my dreams with all that I heard.

As green leaves and blossoms twine and are braided
The strings of my heart have come undone;
When the lush of the green vine is woven unfaded
The binding of my heart with his is as one.

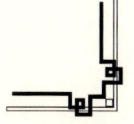

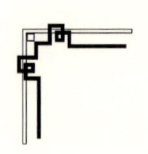

Our Calling

We who've been chosen and heeded the call,
Must not let our reason cause us to fall;
For the god of this world is the master of deceit,
And we ignore warnings in ignorance and conceit.

The cause of all sorrow and sin that became,
The burden we bear, the sorrow we gain;
Is reason we suffer for going our own way,
Not heeding the law, not learning to stay.

We need your strength to light the dark way
Though we are blind we will try to obey;
To you our thoughts and hearts we give
In us we die, in you we live.

We have in our hearts, a promise of grace,
If we walk the strait path and finish the race;
Keep Your hand on me and guide me I pray,
For You are the potter and I am the clay.

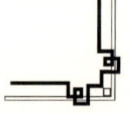

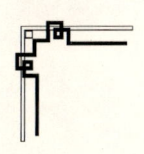

City Life

When roses spill their fragrance,
On summer's joyful day;
And a winding path leads through,
The haunted woodland way;
I remember sadly dreaming,
Of summer's laughing face:
For the city bade me come;
Back to a lonesome place.
I want to see the spider,
Weave on her silken loom;
I want to see the shadows,
Creeping through the gloom;
To find a little butterfly,
Flit with noon's sunbeams;
And look up at the clouds,
That float in azure dreams.
I wish I never had to go,
Back to the busy town;
Where all the empty faces,
Are passing up and down.
Where custom chills the hand,
From a kind and pleasant hold;
And restlessness has taken,
The story never told.
Summer with her lovely way,
Now says good bye to me;
Slowly all the petals fall,
No more sings the bee.
For I had to go back again,
To the dread and dreary town;
Where all the hollow voices,
Echo up and down.

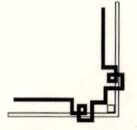

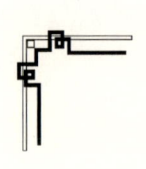

How Could I Tell

I walk no more on soft green mosses,
Under the tree where green branch tosses;
Where scent of leaf and red rose swinging,
Perfumes the wind with soft scent clinging.

I walk no more by the ocean dreaming,
Where sunbeams fly with grey gulls screaming;
Over the cliffs where wild waves falling,
Sweep up the sound with echoes calling.

I hear no more the sea shell's story,
Along the shore with sunset's glory;
Only the song from the dark cave's hollow,
That siren song I dare not follow.

Words you spoke left me broken hearted,
For now I find you have departed.
I loved you well but you left me lonely,
How could I tell if you loved me only?

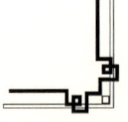

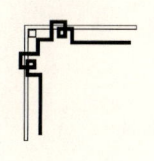

The Party

The host was the most, an elegant man,
Who throws great parties like no one else can.
All were dressed to the nines for a special affair,
While men peeked at bosoms and tried not to stare.

The gathering together of local folks,
Were sitting and telling some witty jokes;
While ladies who came dressed in the latest style,
Vied with each other for a gentleman's smile.

Candles were lit, the music played low,
The table was set in perfection's glow;
With goblets of wine and bone china plates,
That defined the mind with earnest debates.

The fragrance of food that smelled so fine,
Was delivered with bottles of sweet scented wine;
And great steaming bowls of chicken soup,
Were served with a sterling silver scoop.

Roast beef with gravy was served with care,
With mashed potatoes and all the fanfare.
There were squash, carrots and dishes of beans,
And bowls of crisp chopped salad greens.

There was wine to sip and coffee to drink,
There was so much to eat, no one could think;
There was cake to splurge and gin to purge,
And all who ate quickly lost the urge.

The hours ticked by with buttons undone,
That belied the gourmet from having fun;
For lessons they learned were simple and few,
A waist filled with haste is hard to undo.

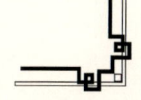

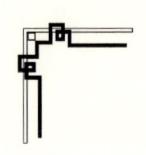

You Live In Me

I shall live in your legend to make
A new spirit now wholly begotten;
For in death, your memory will not forsake
Those words in my soul that are not forgotten.
Your face glows immortal in my heart to save
Even me, for I go too where all must die;
When I would sleep alone in a silent grave
With my love entombed, there you lie.
Your memory will be my triumphant verse
Which my mind has not created yet to read;
And a voice will sing of you to rehearse
Words of praise when the world must heed.
In my heart you live by the stroke of my pen
And I breathe for you through the mouths of men.

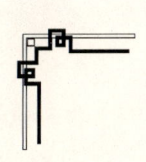

Illusion

Touch the threads of my illusion,
Let's taste the flavor and pretend;
That we are hidden in seclusion,
With words we speak that know no end.

Sing a song of sunlit days,
And sip the taste of heaven's wine;
See a mist through noonday's haze,
Forget the tunes that hinder time.

Take my hand and help me see,
Joy that mingles with light;
Break the chains to set me free,
And clear a mist that blinds my sight.

Close your eyes slip into sleep;
Time to dream with peace of mind.
Drift into forever, fathom the deep,
Arms of rest are always kind.

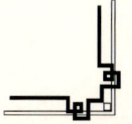

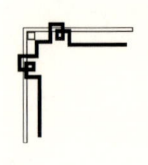

Pathways

Where pathways probe the lonesome place,
And foxes tease with tails to chase;
Rabbits crouch beneath the hedges,
And grey mice play amongst the sedges.

Frogs that squat on rocks in streams,
Croak their songs to pipe their dreams;
While butterflies drift where faeries hide,
And sunbeams dance while shadows died.

Beneath the scented boughs that hang,
To cover hill where bluebells rang;
The lithesome deer with downy fawn,
Flick their tails and now are gone.

A raccoon sits with lonely musing,
Looking with care his food for choosing;
And floating through some jaded dream,
A blue jay squawks her rowdy scream.

Along the path where willows weep,
There hides a nest where owls sleep;
And perilous flight of fleet winged swallow,
Chases light within the hollow.

Silken threads that spiders spin,
Gives hope to catch the fly within;
And squirrels that look with elfin glance,
Perform in trees, their spritely dance.

Across the meadow shadows creep,
Inviting rest, to summon sleep;
And crickets sing their evening song,
To say good bye to a day that's gone.

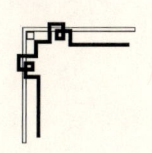

Introspection

Why do my poems lack new thought?
For the theme never seems to change;
Why each day do I look for words sought
To bring diverse meanings that aren't strange?
I seem to be captive to feelings all the same
And don't carry my words in another dream;
For what I write almost speaks my name
And brings light to my secret gleam,
Showing how my inner soul created
The words of love I speak for you;
For indeed dear, we two are mated
And all that was old is now new.
For as the earth renews from new to old,
So my love for you again needs to be told.

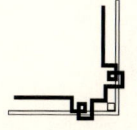

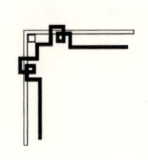

My Garden

Blow your breath through my garden
Wind of the western sea;
Tell my love to come swiftly
And bring a rose to me.
There on the dew dropped flowers
Rests a soft grey dove;
And I wait at the garden gate
For the footsteps of my love.

I will come through the garden with haste
Where the rose is scenting the way;
And open the gate for my lover
When he comes to stay.
I dream of the look on his face
I wait for the sound of his feet;
Here in the dew of the garden
It is magic when we meet.

Don't blow your breath on the mountain
Storm of the cold cruel north;
Bring the wind of the west for healing
Gather her skirts and come forth.
Spread perfume and sweet honey
Spill your aromas of spice;
For him who came to my garden
And took me to paradise.

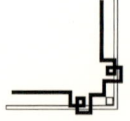

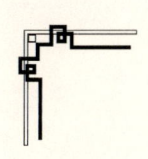

Luminous Lady

At midnight in the month of May
The mystic moon took light from day;
A gauzy mist so white and dim,
Breathes a sigh from her silver rim.
Softly dropping drip by drip,
She paints a petal of the violet's lip;
Taking her mist over valley and lake,
Bringing sleep for my baby's sake.

Oh luminous lady of the night,
Cast your stars thru shimmering light;
Bring phantom shadows to rise and fall,
On stones that cover the garden wall.
Ride the night with your pallid eye,
And light the ghosts as they fly;
Let the lyrics of ancient folklore,
Bring your echo here once more.

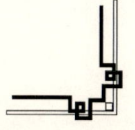

Sleep

Little sorrows sigh and weep,
To keep awake those who'd sleep.
Memories past seem to surround,
And all that is cannot be found.

But needing rest we toss and turn,
Shedding thoughts as though to learn,
Of a dream forgone, a deed forborne;
To all who take but are given scorn.

So is your misery worth a tear,
Does your sorrow create fear?
Can your thoughts no longer keep,
You having rest and needed sleep?

In the prison of your mind,
Let go the ghosts that seek to bind.
Drift into silence, softly go
And sleep will follow, that I know.

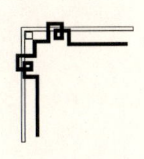

My Love

My love wakes in the morning,
When the birds sing soft to hear;
The day springs from night's dreaming,
And summer's feet swing clear.
Life scampers through the meadows,
Daisies bloom beneath her feet;
The stream flows through the woodland,
With a song that is so sweet.
Branches laden with the fruit,
So low a limb could hold;
As harvest filled with plenty,
For a king in his treasure fold.
Life danced with all the shadows,
That were cast by substance fair;
My love laughed in the morning,
As she sweetly lingered there.

Now she sleeps there in the twilight,
And my heart is filled with fear;
Her laughter lost in darkness,
And my joy died in a tear.
I whispered, "Rest while I am singing",
When shadows come at night;
Each fair blossom swinging,
With faint perfumed delight.
When the world is filled with laughter,
And the lark flies on the wing;
When man calls to the hereafter,
There's no song left there to sing.
Her life faded to a shadow,
Death loved her body fair;
My love smiled in her sleeping,
With no one but me to care.

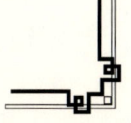

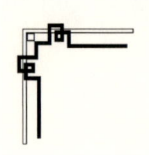

Sonnet on Leaving

I'd like to see the empty years,
Through my bewildered eyes;
And bathe my fingertips in tears,
And give silence when love dies.
I'd stroll through sunlit meadows,
And knock at the picket gate.
To stand beneath dark shadows,
Accepting the hand of fate;
How clear I see and true to say,
With love's unbending rule;
That one shall weep and one shall stray,
Accepting life is cruel
Now that I'm the first to go,
I'm content it happened so.

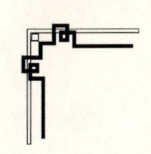

Summer

So many problems to rile the day
And troubles to haunt the nights;
My mind had all but forgotten
Old passions and sweet delights.
Then summer came in the arms of June
In beauty, wonder and mirth
She hung the stars about the moon
And rained sunshine on the earth.
She poured the rain and burst the bud
Then lit the rose with fire;
She stirred again my brooding blood
And gave me new desire.

Nights were aglow with jewelled skies
The days were bursting with song;
And all the dreams she did devise
Healed pain and eased the wrong.
On top of hill or deep in dell
When the streams goes rushing by
My pulse would surge and swell
My heart would throb and sigh.
I felt his heart beat with my own
I drank the sweetness of his breath;
Till my fears and time had flown
And we had no fear of death.

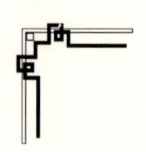

The Dancing Girl

A blithe young girl with lively feet,
Said she would rather dance than eat;
So she shook off all the worldly blues,
And put on her dancing shoes.
She danced thru day and danced thru night,
She danced till the stars lost their light;
She danced her lover out of breath,
And danced her husband quite to death.
She danced all her beauty away,
And then she danced the night away;.
At last her big toe went out of joint,
And all the others came to a point.
Still she danced, and waltzed and whirled,
The dizziest girl in all the world.
She danced herself like a spinning top,
Out of breath but could not stop;
Still whirling around, she flew so far,
Her feet got caught on the point of a star:
And there she danced for all to see,
In all the dark spaces of eternity.

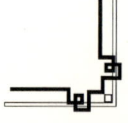

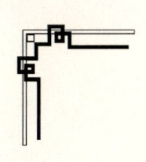

Under the Sun

Who treads the high places on the earth,
Who gave our planet joy in rebirth?
Who turns the shadow of death into morning,
Who turned transgression into mourning?

Increased knowledge increases sorrow,
With all that we carry into tomorrow;
For in wisdom there's always much grief,
To scar a mind with our unbelief.

We need His wisdom to guide our heart,
To take what we have and set us apart.
All is in vain, just grasping the wind,
All we look for is not easy to find.

Even at night the heart takes no rest,
We've lost the way with all that was blessed;
That which is done is what will be done,
For there is nothing new under the sun

Unto everything there is a new season,
So we stop to search the reason;
For God is in heaven and we upon earth
So we need to accept all that has worth.

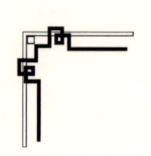

We cannot remember that which was,
For we have forsaken God's precious laws;
Nor will we remember all that will come,
For all things are evil under the sun.

God has no pleasure in vacant fools,
Who go their own way and forsake His rules;
Therefore let all of your words be few,
And may all our actions help to renew.

Like shadows passing through days of life,
Coming with silence and bringing much strife;
Then that which profits those seeing the sun,
Is all that gives true life to everyone.

The race isn't to swift or battle to strong,
For things that divide us from right and wrong;
I considered in my heart all of these things,
For sorrow and sadness that evil brings.

Like thoughts that pass through weary years,
Coming in silence, bringing shed tears;
The memory's forgotten, it has no share,
For we've been deceived and caught in the snare.

From the book of Ecclesiastes

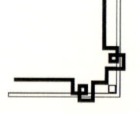

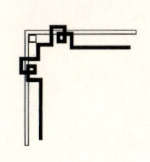

Spring Is Late

So long winter held her in his arms,
So long we waited for spring's sunny charms;
We dreamed of that time when all the flowers,
Would bring the scent that was only ours.

The promise came slowly but we wait,
For winter lingers and spring's too late;
But forces that lie silent in the earth
Will soon bring the breath of spring to birth.

She brings her song through green meadows,
Hiding her light in soft shadows;
She awakens all the drowsy flowers,
That slept so long in winter's lonely hours.

Through the dried leaves the violets push up,
The crocus awakens and the buttercup;
Then daffodils rise and daisies play,
In fields where so late the snowflakes lay.

She brings her light to touch with gold,
The song she sings no one else has told;
For in the heart there's a gift to bring,
In springtime's snow and winter's spring.

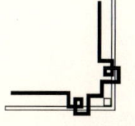

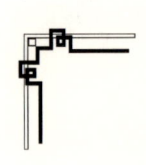

The Dance

The man in Berlin loves to dance
By the mist of the soft evening moon;
He takes his time to step on the rhyme
But he never found the tune.
There's a street where nobody goes
Where sad echoes bounce off the walls;
Where shadows march to the drum of woes
And crawl fast down the lonely halls.

You know dear I want you, I do,
I need to lie down with you soon
When the leaves on the tree are so few
I wait when love whispers a tune.
There's a slice torn out of the sky
And day's scented with lilies of snow;
The weary birds find it hard to fly
For they're scattered with nowhere to go.

There's a music hall in Berlin
Where notes play loud to reviews;
There's a bar where no one is talking
They're condemned to death by the blues.
When will they look at your picture
And see the lost lonely years?
Come hold me my darling and dance
To the music of fantastic tears.

I'll dance with you in Berlin
I'll be dressed in laughter's disguise;
With red roses between my breasts
And my hand caressing your thighs.
I'll yield to your aura of beauty
And see what you've got chained to tomorrow;
It will never be just a duty
To love you without all my sorrow.

A reflection on the Second World War

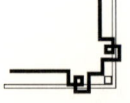

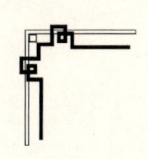

A Royal Birth

A star in the east shining bright,
Brought three kings through the dark of night;
Bearing gifts for a child just born,
As the star in the east brought a new morn.

They travelled nights and many days,
Through arid desert and woodland ways;
By azure sea and shore land meadows,
In scorching sun and cool dark shadows.

Yet with trust they followed the star,
The way was hard and very far;
At last they came where the baby lay,
No crown had he, no place to stay.

But in a stable he came to be,
And three kings bowed on bended knee
One brought gold to crown His head;
One brought frankincense to scent His bed.

The last brought myrrh for his hour of need,
When those who sought him did their deed.
And the angels flew with moonshine wing,
Bringing to shepherds, visions of a King.

They praised the day when Christ was born,
Who appeared a child that blessed morn.

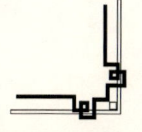

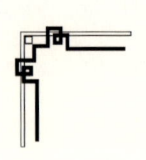

The Gift

God gave a little child
He gave this child to me;
The babe was made with love,
His soul was made by Thee.
His face a sunny blossom,
His body fair and bright,
The halo of his hair,
Was raven as the night.
This child is a part of me,
This gift of flesh divine;
And all the world was bright and new,
With this precious gift of mine.
Dear Father let me give you praise,
To share him with you all his days.

The Heart is Deceitful

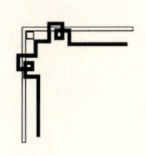

The heart is deceitful above all things,
Desperately corrupt in its way;
It takes one down a devious path,
And leads the lost to go astray.

We who live on this earthly ground,
Are those who live where peace isn't found;
We need to soothe the thoughts that spring,
Out of human suffering.

The deeds we do we soon forget,
But heaven's record is firmly set;
But those who pursue planned perfection,
Will rise to greet a new direction.

We shall reap what we sow,
And find the place where sinners go,
Or ask for mercy so we can find,
Healing we need for a troubled mind.

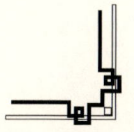

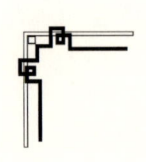

You do Not Know

You don't know it, but I would hear
One word of love from you;
There is no ache I would not bear,
I would do all for you.

I could carefully toil all the day,
My weary feet could run;
If only at the end you could say,
"I love you dearest one".

You don't know it, but to win
Appreciation from your eyes;
My soul has conquered many a sin,
But not my troubled cries.

You do not know how bold and strong
A woman's heart can be true;
But few could hide the pain so long,
That mine has held from you.

So if I have this one sweet chance,
To meet your eye dear friend;
Would you scorn it with a careless glance,
Or know to whom I penned.

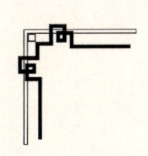

Wildflowers

Larkspur blooming in the garden,
With violets in the dell;
Ask to beg some pardon,
Because their petals fell.

Roses climbing on the wall,
Reach up to find the light;
While lilies standing oh so tall,
Have throats that sing delight.

Columbine is reaching up,
Her colours sigh in vain;
And campanula lifts her cup,
To drink the falling rain.

The sunny shades of gold trefoil,
Are basking in the sun;
While hyacinths send scented oil,
To delight the nose of everyone.

Blue phlox lifts her lovely locks,
To sigh upon the breeze;
While poppies grow in scarlet flocks,
Their fires can but please.

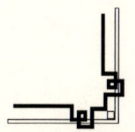

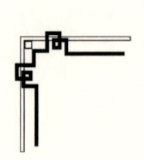

Purple coneflower spreads her petals,
Around a browny head;
And hanging heads of soft bluebells,
Are like a blanket spread.

The goldenrod stands in the sun,
Bringing songbirds there to sing;
And asters bloom for everyone,
To beckon the butterfly wing.

The spreading spikes of bergamot,
Give honey to the bees;
And geraniums sit and think a thought,
Beneath the leafy trees.

Flowers come in many shades,
Their glory finds a place;
To soon the scented petal fades,
To soon the blooms erase.

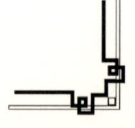

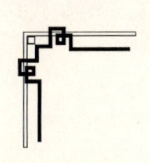

Shadows

We are but lonesome shadows it's true,
We pay the debt that's always due;
But scorn the years of no return,
And weep the tears that never learn.

There are lives to live and deaths to die,
Stories to tell and tears to cry;
For when all the willful souls have strayed,
Flesh and blood will surely fade.

When light and air become as one,
Giving grace to a brilliant sun;
Then we fly a message across the sky,
To hasten the hour when wings can fly.

When you are close and I am near,
Then clocks tick back to yesteryear;
And in my heart love blooms to sing,
With summer's snow and winter's spring.

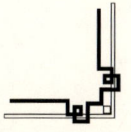

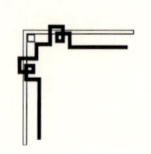

Old and Gray

In glad surprise I blink my eyes
And hail the rosy morn;
Before the diamond dewdrop dries,
With shimmer on the thorn.
When on the branch the robins sing,
And bees hum with the day;
I'm feeling youth with joy of spring,
But I am old and gray.

But when no more I feel the joy,
In the urgency of that hour;
With fleet of foot a happy boy,
I play with the meadow's flower.
When the spice is gone and I don't feel,
To greet a brand new day;
Then know I'm old and let me steal,
From other folks away.

But now I waken with a smile,
And sit under the laurel tree;
For there is only a little while,
Of life that's left in me.
But when night comes I fade away
Where lonely feet walk far;
To find that light to show the way,
And awaken with a star.

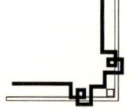

Ghost Lady

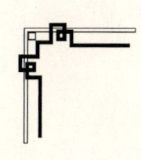

She is the pale ghost
That rides the dark night;
Where wanders the spirit
Soundless and white.

Through the waves of the sea
Through the echoes of space;
There finds a wan image
That reflects a dead face.

When down through the ages
Was her beginning?
What is her legend
What was her sinning?

Do all throngs of angels
Discern her sweet crime?
Does it emerge in the vapour
In the arms of time?

Does she spin in an orbit
With never a sound?
Does she laugh in her place
With the stars all around?

Disfigured and marred
Empty and old;
A heart found now hard
A memory grown cold.

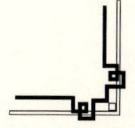

New Year

I heard the chimes at twelve o'clock
Ring in a brand new year;
And beyond the noise of all the news
I listened hard to hear
A chorus of lamentation
Ringing loud and singing clear
From many angels winging
Through the vault of heaven.
They sang of shame and sorrow
Of suffering and sin;
They sang of hope for tomorrow
That peace be found and guided in.

I knew of all the many trials
That former years had cost;
And all the dreams and pleasures
That were wasted then and lost.
With awe I heard the music
That came to me there;
The voices all came pealing
Through the stillness everywhere.
"Take away the shame and sorrow
Take the suffering and sin
So that a new tomorrow
May find peace be guided in".

Then I offered up a prayer
With heartfelt words I pled
For a miracle for the living
And forgiveness for the dead.
Then the echoes of the music
Softly whispered as songs were sung
They came with phantom voices
From the joyful angel's tongue
"Take away the grief and sorrow
Of suffering and sin;
And in that new tomorrow
Let peace be found within".

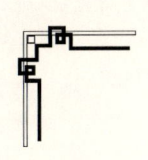

Tears to Weep

When I lay me down to sleep,
And cry the tears that sinners weep,
I speak the words of a contrite prayer,
And know that someone listens there.

He cares for sheep that have gone astray,
Who willfully wander their own way;
They vex the pride that hides within,
And drink the bitter cup of sin.

The web of lies and dark deception,
Lie in defeat of Light's conception;
To capture all and destroy life,
With passion's fire and human strife.

We need to plant the gospel vine,
Where evil rules and saints repine;
Where martyrs lead with ransomed prayer,
With hope for life that tarries there.

Blood that was shed on Calvary,
Set slaves of transgression wholly free;
So we rise from the grave to seek reward,
Giving praise to a living Lord.

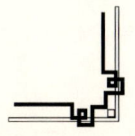

A New Day

Fingers of dawn bring dewdrops falling,
Tears for a brand new day;
A rose coloured sky brings the lark calling
A song she sings to bright May.
The lilac is bending in her royal color,
Lost in the purple of night;
Star shine is softer and duller,
A new day brings life's delight.

Open the window and bend above me
Dearest red rose, my sweet song;
Shed your thorns if you love me
For nights without you are so long.
The day is ours, and daylight is breaking
Sweet drowsy eyes of grey;
You won't question an early waking
When the wings of night fly away.

Bring Me Water

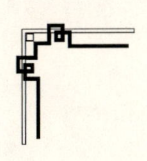

Bring me water to wash my stain,
Wash me clean with showers of rain;
For all I need is something new,
The need is great, Your gift is true.

Give me water to wash my fears,
For my walk through life shed many tears,
Although that walk was long and far,
At last I'm finding where You are.

Give me relief for great is my sorrow,
Your infinite mercy I need to borrow;
Lest I sigh but hope in vain,
To partake of sorrow's pain.

Give me Your blood to wash within,
My grievous pride and mortal sin,
I need to turn and try my best,
It is only then I'll find my rest.

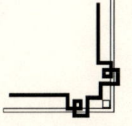

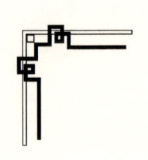

City Garden

I know a haven dear and fair,
That's downtown in the city square;
Where sweet rows of perfumed bloom,
Lies surrounded by soot and gloom;
Right in the center of the bustling town,
Like a shining jewel of harlot's gown.
A plaintive cry from the tulip bed,
Whispered in my ear and said;
"Here in the heart of noise and strife,
We live a humble, simple life.
Here surrounded by evil and shame,
We do what we can with our crimson flame;
We dance in the wind with blossom and grace,
To make the city a lovlier place.
So good it is though the place is vile,
That through the grime and smoke we smile;
Many the people that pass by there,
By the tulips that bloom in the city square;
Listens with sorrow to the tulips plight,
Wishing them another place out of sight.

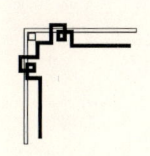

My Song to You

Come to the meadow just you only,
Where autumn weaves her spell;
On hills and purple moorlands lonely,
Where the magic of her presence dwells.

Beneath blue sky and fields of heather,
With soft humming of honey bees.
And I'll hold you, just us two together,
To share the scent of autumns leaves.

We've time to share asters in the meadow,
With all that we love best;
With the swallows wings and your shadow,
And summer's grass that built the nest.

To hold and hear the soft wind singing,
To see your hair tossed and blown;
And meet the bluebird softly winging,
Through heaven and earth, we too fly alone.

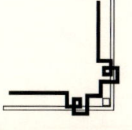

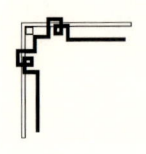

How Green the Valley

How green was our valley
Down in the dell;
We took time to dally,
Under its spell.
To look at the flowers,
That dance through the day;
To greet the cool showers,
That come here to play.
And through all the fields,
The bright poppies wave;
Bowing to honor,
Another new grave.
Nestled in clumps,
Where sweet violets lie;
Reflecting the haze,
Of a twilight sky.
They weep with the dewdrops,
From off of their stems;
Perpetual teardrops,
Falling like gems.

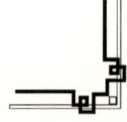

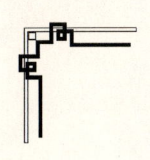

Lives to Live

I need more lives for me to live
In this universe of beauty;
I plan more days to find new ways
Of doing freedom's duty.
I need not more joy than this
For I am life's dear lover;
And when I wage to turn the page
I'd never want another.

The glorious pledge of sunny Spring
With sweet June coming after;
Bring autumn sighs and summer's cries
Lost in winter's laughter.
With virgin moon and scorching noon's
And stars of a thousand nights;
I'd need no heaven if love be given
With all its sweet delights.

There are many splendors for the eye
And such music for the ear;
The mind would reel with all to feel
And see to touch and hear.
There's many ways to spend the days
And more to do what's kind;
For bread now cast on waters past
Returns again I find.

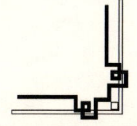

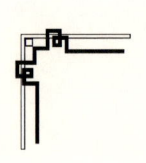

There are such gifted souls to know
And many more to learn;
While a promise rests in earth's warm breast
And unknown stars still burn.
In six days God made all the earth
The bible is known to say;
Six lives I need to plant a seed
Of love, with one for each dear day.

But sad if love should fly away
Or hide his face from me;
Six lives aren't much if I had such
But one's all that need be.
With unhappy May and sorry June
Cold dawns and a weary night;
A sorry world through space was hurled
When love had lost her light.

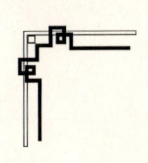

Stormy Waters

I love to be me and that's a good sign,
When the wind is flying with this heart of mine;
It taps at the window with cold mournful chill,
Chasing the leaves that dance down the hill.

The sky's dark and cloudy, a sea white with foam,
And seagulls screaming as they fly back home;
The boat is wild tossing as she flies in the gale,
To rise on the waves as the wind fills her sail.

I'm just a woman trapped here on shore,
A soul that is longing for each breaker's roar;
The heart beats restless with the winds that blow,
Where ever she flies is where I want to go.

The gulls fly the heavens far beyond shore,
Winging the skies with clouds evermore;
Fly with the tempest a gypsy heat true,
There's joy in the peril as you fly in the blue.

The oceans that thunder lift dark waves to pray,
And tempests that shriek take the breath away;
The foam that flies will cover the land,
And take the small footprint from out of the sand.

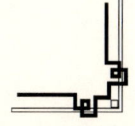

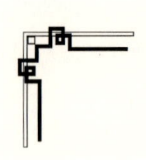

Ghosts

How silent are the dead,
Whose quiet feet don't stray;
We see them face to face,
As they go their lonely way.

These ghostly apparitions,
Who've forgotten all their fears;
They rebuke our aching heart,
And fill our time with tears.

Beside the flickering fire,
They steal the vacant chair;
They glide all through the house,
Passing silent up the stair.

When comes the fall of night,
And we are called to sleep;
Around our head in dreams,
These ghostly spirits creep.

In dark forbidden hours,
Their sighing rides the storm;
They whisper to the wind,
With voices so forlorn.

How elusive are the dead,
Who hear our anxious call;
They float throughout the dark,
And answer not at all.

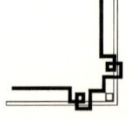

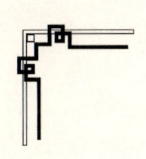

I Am

I heard the vesper winds
Within the flickering fire;
This world is not forever
Knowing lost trust and desire.

I am the love of mortal
The longing for all things;
I am the glow of summer
I am the sweep of wings.

I am the tender longing
That's there before the thought;
The praise and adoration
In which our dreams are sought.

Scattered on the field
I call the tiny seed;
There the leaf and flower
Arise to meet my need.

Within the fading embers
I fan the dying spark;
To make the hearts of lovers
Light their flame when dark.

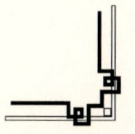

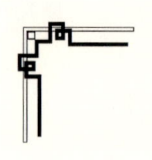

Time

I am naught and you are all,
You are grand and I am small;
Our lives hold time with joy and sorrow,
Hovering between today and tomorrow.

A time to rise and a time to fall,
A space to feel nothing at all;
For time touches all that is real,
And nothing at all is what time tries to steal

A time to work, a time to play,
Time comes to greet another day;
Needing to touch the earth and sky,
To find the key to the question why.

Time to feel joy, time to feel pain,
To touch all we feel all over again;
For joy brings life and happy laughter,
But pain brings tears and often anger.

Time to climb with stilts to Mars,
To play in the blue with all the stars;
Skipping through heaven's bright Milky Way,
While others sleep and others play.

Time to love spring, time to love fall,
If I had to choose I'd take them all;
For spring brings life with birds that nest,
And autumn brings a soft season of rest.

A time to be born, and a time to die,
A time to laugh, and a time to cry;
The young at heart have lives to live,
And the grey haired old have lives to give.

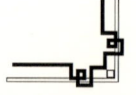

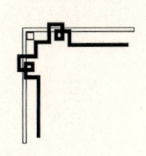

A Season

How bright the sun of summer shines
Through fields and soaring pines;
And gentle winds go passing by
Above a sky of sapphire blue'
Around bright blossom's brilliant hue
To enchant the passerby.

But what were those pleasures to me
When I considered a memory
That came softly drifting by?
I closed my eyes and dreamed away
All the cares that disturbed the day
From earth and air and sky.

The hyacinth's sweet fragrance dwells
With bright mounds of brave blue bells;
With miles and miles of nodding flowers
With all the daisies dancing still
Spreading lace upon the hill
To delight all my idle hours.

But these joys have come and gone
For these glories come not alone;
The sun must halo all that's past
Not all lovely; the painful grief
Although its time be brief
Is bitter while it last.

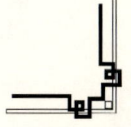

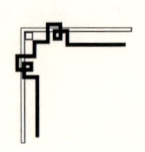

Tender Moments

All of the tender moments we shared,
When you held my hand and told me you cared;
Bring to each day a new fascination,
With lips to kiss, a heart filled with elation.
Come lie with me in fields of sweet clover,
Where honey bees fly and the scent hovers over;
Where all we feel is always new,
And minutes are plenty but the hours are few.
Let me hold you close and look in your eyes,
And speak all the words my heart denies;
For when I hold you near I can feel my heart,
Beating each moment till we have to part.
And as we walk our ways into the setting sun,
The parting of ways will merge into one.

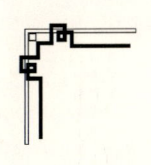

Temptation

In the darkness of midnight and despair,
When I toss and turn in my bed;
With tears and memories I err,
Down the pathway of sin I have fled.
In my mind there are visions I'd banish,
Of truths of the deeds I have done;
For I beg and ask that they vanish,
And they vanish, all except one.

That one with a sigh like the splendor,
Of the moon in the midnight skies;
That one with a magic so tender.
That one with a trance in his eyes.
He comes close in his loving beauty,
With languid, indolent grace;
And my heart won't do its duty,
When I look at the light in his face.

He caresses my face and I quiver,
And tremble with exquisite pains;
He sighs like the wind on the river,
And blood rushes fast through my veins.
He half smiles in amorous fashion,
And kisses with soft tender touch,
He holds me with power and passion,
In his arms I love him so much.

Oh phantoms of sad unrelenting,
Fly back to the darkness and sod;
Always too dear for repenting,
He stands between me and my God.
If by an oath I should meet him,
And kiss those lips I love well;
So dear in my arms I would greet him,
And melt in the fires of hell.

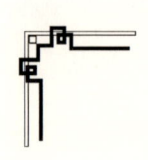

Change

Nothing's the same, all things change
And I find I don't love you the same old way;
I'll be your friend for all is not estranged
If you happen to come today.

The excitement that made my life a dream
The ecstasy of that time, the serene content;
Like a whisper of a sleeper's mind it would seem
Is a mystery as to how it went.

The birds, the blossoms and leaves on the trees
The cold white moon who rides sublime;
The transient breath, the eternal seas
All things change with the dance of time.

Our face in the mirror shows year after year
The signs of age; and our expectant need
Ignores the hope now drowned in a tear
Carrying all we knew but did not heed.

Can we ask the mortal heart to stay
And be happy with a child's sweet hours?
The season says goodbye to the violets of May
And knows there are no fairer flowers.

But life holds no dearer love than this
Which rests in peace but cold and dumb;
But let us kiss and oh, how we will miss
The violets that change when the roses come.

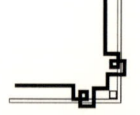

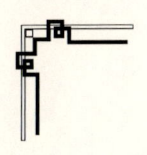

His Nose

The nose he wears sits on his head
It's big and round and very red;
And in the dark it always glows
It must be awful to own that nose.
There's two dark holes filled with hair
With whatever else that's hidden there;
Each time I see with great surprise
That glow that sits between his eyes.
It shines as though when night meets day
There never could be another way;
I wonder too if he can tell
If red affects his sense of smell.
Perhaps the problem is I think
He's had in time too much to drink;
I suggested then to paint it white
And he seemed to think this was alright.

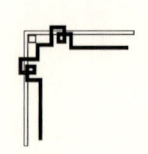

You Are

You are the sun in my morning,
The moonbeams in my night;
You are the cream in my coffee,
The bluebird in my flight.

You are the music in my soul,
The bubbles in my wine;
You are all that makes me whole,
For you I walk the line.

You are the warmth in our embrace,
The starlight in my eyes;
I need reach out to touch your face,
To know what love implies.

You are the reason for my thought
The passion in a kiss;
You are the gentle touch I sought,
A teardrop in the mist.

You are the minute in my time,
A song that needs to sing;
You are the rhythm in my rhyme,
The gold that's in my ring.

You are a dream that wants to stay,
The reason that I smile;
For you are everything to me,
Why I walk that extra mile.

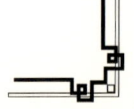

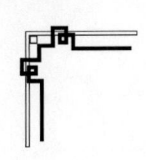

In Dreams

There are nights of silk and tears,
When we realize our fears;
And upon a bed we lie,
Wishing wings could make us fly.

How is it that the things we do,
Holds our sorrow, keeps us blue?
Can we face and say goodbye,
To all the dreams that were a lie?

All is hapless, nothing whole,
For that which pains a hungry soul.
So we reach out in sweet embrace,
Sheltered in a state of grace.

Only in dreams a soul takes flight,
Soaring, blending with the light.
For a soul is but a formality,
That takes the spirit to eternity.

Joy

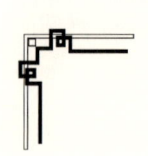

To touch your face, to form a trace,
Lifts up with joyful laughter;
And eyes that gaze on happy days,
Sing songs in the sweet hereafter.

What's in the mind can't be defined,
As I touch your wistful smile;
But lovers may on a bright spring day,
Linger close in their arms awhile.

In an amorous mind we need to remind,
Of dreams that come at night;
But try to find that words need be kind,
If the heart should take its flight.

Should we desire to tread to a leafy bed,
Alone among scented flowers;
To share a kiss, a moment of bliss,
In moonlight's fleeting hours.

To look in your eyes says my body denies,
Emotions that I feel;
But in my heart know we will never part,
For my love for you is real.

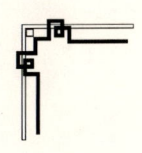

Hands of Time - Sonnet

To me dear love, you will never be old
It is your inner beauty that captivates me;
For in your face so many stories are told
That I contemplate in tranquil reverie.
The short time we shared brings vistas yet unseen
Promises to be discovered within the heart;
Perfumed with tenderness of what comes between
Those vacant hours when we have to part.
You are the treasure that fills my being
Without you I am empty and incomplete;
But together we share that special feeling
That the hands of time will never cheat.
Let's take what we have and make it all come true
Those hours, days and years I would spend with you.

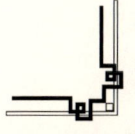

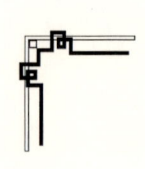

Weariness

She woke to see another day,
Now she wakes to grief;
All the sunny days are gone,
With time that is the thief.

Once she rose to greet the dawn,
Now she hates to rise;
When she needs to greet the day,
She opens tired eyes.

Songbirds in the blossomed tree,
With flowers all unfurled;
Hold dreams that are not to be,
In her other world.

Why would she seek a higher place?
For alone she drifts right here;
Quiet in the nether parts,
With those who held her dear.

When twilight comes they rise,
Each familiar face;
Phantoms floating round her head,
Hold her spirit in embrace.

Now she wakes to greet the day,
To take a brand new breath;
Then recalls her need to sleep,
With the weariness of death.

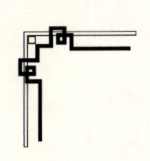

Lover's Knot

A wistful glance upon her face,
Belies the smile I need to trace;
For love needs not cruel rejection,
Instead it longs for sweet perfection.

Reaching out to touch tomorrow,
Leaving all that causes sorrow;
Looking forward with such yearning,
Finding joy at your returning.

Let me taste your scent once more,
Bring back the dream we had before;
Have no fear and fear no scorn.
For buds of love will soon be born.

On your cheek the morning blush,
On your brow a fevered flush;
Like berries sitting in the cream,
You light my soul and fill my dream.

Let me quench your thirsty lips,
And taste the juice of honeyed drips;
To caress the languid eyes that sleep,
And join with mine that need to weep.

I need reach out to touch a star,
To know for sure just where you are;
For body language is understood,
Giving and forgiving all it should.

When fingers knit a lovers knot,
And find a stitch that they forgot;
Then all things that transpire,
Will feed the flame that lights the fire.

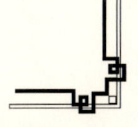

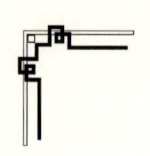

Contrary Thoughts

Laugh and the world laughs with you
Cry and you cry alone;
The natives of earth must steal their mirth
Or be sad and be all alone.
Speak and the mountains will call
Sigh and sound flies on the air;
Echoes rebound with a mournful sound
As they float in the nebulous air.

Be happy and mankind will pursue you
Sorrow will drive them away;
They need the pleasure of all your leisure
But don't need your stories of grey.
Speak joy and your companions are many
With grief there's not many at all;
For there's nothing so fine as a sip of wine
But alone you will stumble and fall.

Celebrate and your table is gathered
Fast and the world will sigh;
Perfection to give will show how to live
But alone you must learn to die.
There is space in the soul for pleasure
There is space in the heart for rain;
But when it's begun look for the sun
Through the dark passage of pain.

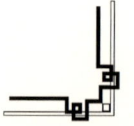

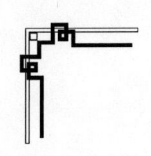

Lost Memories

We drank a glass of crimson wine
We drank to long lost days;
Where in the past sweet memories shine
When our love was all ablaze.
But seasons died and visions fade
With phantoms of love's lost dream;
The joys we knew have never stayed
They sleep within this ruby stream.

We picked the purple grapes that lay
Beneath the brilliance of the sun;
Where the shimmer of an autumn day
Was reflected where the waters run.
We hoarded all the clustered shapes
That brought old times conjured up;
Of feet that danced upon the grapes
And wine that filled the chalice cup.

Within these drops of crimson lie
Blushing shackles holding fast;
Those dancing shadows that can't die
Brought fleet winged dreams that hurry past.
We touched the goblet's silver rim
Each sip adored the grape's sweet stain;
Then bubbles sprang from the brim
To assault the spaces of the brain.

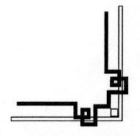

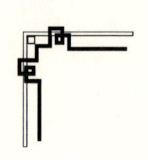

Pride

There is this thing called foolish pride,
A sorry affair hides deep inside;
For willful souls that know no song,
Stubborn as the day is long.

It drives away who care the most,
And hurts the mind with idle boast;
They may be on top but will soon be alone,
When the fault is theirs alone.

For pride's the easy way to fall,
They never listen or heed the call;
All that mattered was a selfish need,
To rise o'er others with willful greed.

Before it's late and time marches on,
Turn away before the chance is gone;
Consider the time as you make your bed,
It's a lonely place to lay your head.

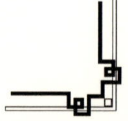

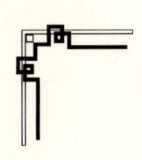

Searching

When I'm thinking pro and con,
Of dreams my love is built upon;
A willing mouth, to be kissed,
A curious mind, a lovely twist;
Of speech as ancient as first sin,
With shell like ear and dimpled chin.
With shapely limbs and deep dark eyes,
That look at me as though they're wise.
When I sit and think apart,
Of all I need to fill my heart;
Empty trifles don't trouble me,
They make me glad for normalcy.

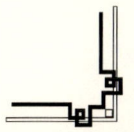

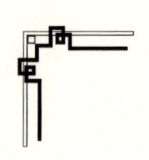

How Should I know

My pretty child how should I know,
How cold the winter's blight would blow;
To draw you in with such despair,
When he sought your presence there.
How a lonely lady should come and go,
When love had left, how could she know?

How might I know, my dear child,
When lovely springtime looked and smiled?
Gentle the nodding roses breath,
Who never knew the trance of death.
Like she who stood in glad surprise,
When she imagined love in your eyes;
I didn't know time could so swiftly pass,
As shadows that dance across the grass.

My darling child, how would I know,
How long I watched you come and go;
How I waited to see you for so long,
When all that happened was so wrong.
You came to me in a gown so white,
And filled the silence of my night;
I looked but found one lonely star,
And knew how far heaven's gardens are.

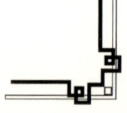

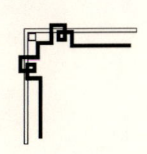

Ancestry

It was my ancestors who gave me
My spirit's glowing flame;
The image of grace, and an angels face
And the message of my name.

But it was all the men I loved
And not my ancient sires
Who put in my heart a flickering flame
And the dazzling rainbow fires.

I always wanted more from them
Than they were willing to give;
But now we go our separate ways
Each with different lives to live.

As the wreckage now is burning
That's found in the crimson blaze;
There shines in the sky's blue splendor
Sweeter and brighter days.

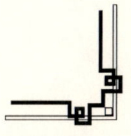

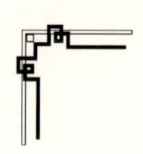

The Shadow and the Song

Out of the mists of twilight,
Into the noonday sun;
Slender limbs and brown eyed,
Dances my lovely one.

She skips through the meadow singing,
Her shadow frolics along;
Which of these should I follow,
The shadow or the song.

I followed her dancing shadow,
Where love gives heart to all;
Then I captured the song,
Where echoes cease to call.

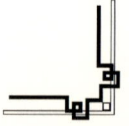

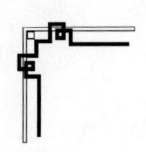

Tragedy

The field is wet with sunshine,
Ripe grasses green and high;
With a reaper in the meadow,
And a bird flies in the sky.

There's a nest with little babies,
With three beaks opened wide;
A reaper's in the meadow,
And a song hangs in the sky.

The meadow's ripe with summer,
And a tragedy passes by;
With a scythe in the meadow,
And a song up in the sky.

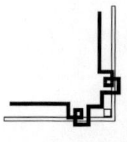

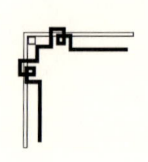

Dreamland

When my child lies on her pillow,
To close her eyes and dream.
She drifts away with stars to play,
Where magic paints the scene.

Mermaids with their tresses wild,
Dance beneath the sea;
And dolphins sing their vesper hymn,
Beneath the coral tree.

Faeries dance in filmy gowns,
In woodlands dark and deep;
With stars to trim their silver crowns,
While blossoms rest in sleep.

She dreamt of a pixie painter,
And watched as the vision grew;
A violet smiled beside him,
As he dipt his brush in dew.

He painted all to please the mind,
The shades of earth and sky;
The buds of all the roses,
And the light in a blue bird's eye.

At last the dawn is breaking,
Rosy sunrise paints the skies;
My darling is awakening,
As she rubs her sleepy eyes.

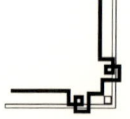

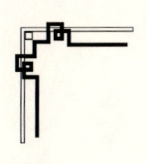

Neurosis

I go by myself walking
I hear myself talking;
Then as I deliberate
On the direction of my fate
That leaves me so anxious
With illusions atrocious
Invading my privacy
With the blight of absurdity.
It comes there unbidden
Like troubles forbidden;
Showing weird faces
In my secret places;
Peevish and fractious
Mindless and anxious
Blighting the laughter
With deeds that come after;
Trying to taunt me
To follow and haunt me.
In my mind they come festering
In my ears they are pestering
That my enemies are treacherous
My friends are ominous
And my life is dangerous.
The calamitous confusions
Bring perfidious allusions
Deceptions so diabolical
Fears that are comical.
And all these do vex me
With nightmares to perplex me
While Satan sits amused
Knowing I am confused

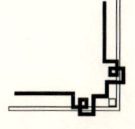

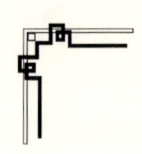

The Rooster

A rooster stood there with his fluted crown,
Wondering which way he'd go out on the town;
He had an evil eye and with lust there was no lack,
As he gazed on the hens he was wont to attack.
His intent was to choose the easiest to find,
And with passionate wing he'd paddle her behind;
But the hens were wary of his stealthy advance,
And fear was there in each anxious glance.
There was no love for he was no friend,
And the attack was bitter right to the end;
There were scuffles and shuffles and bruised feathered wing,
With cawing and clawing and no chicken to sing.
He flattened her there in the cloudy dust,
While his passions were consumed with a rigorous lust;
And the poor little hen sat looking dazed,
While the rooster stalked off proud of his ways.
I guess that's the nature of the nasty bird,
He's best in a soup pot where his noise won't be heard.

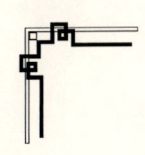

The Mermaid

I pulled her from the waves,
And brought her to the shore;
A mermaid I never caught,
So sweet in my net before.
Soft she was as the foam,
That sails on the white capped sea,
I took her in my arms,
Where I longed for her to be.
I held her close to my heart,
And I kissed her salt wet cheek;
She looked into my eyes,
To hear words of love I speak.
I sang to make her happy,
I was glad to see her play;
And well we loved and laughed,
Throughout the live long day.
Yet my joy was not to last,
In her hand she had a shell;
She held it to her ear,
And heard the ocean's swell.
She heard the cry of the sea,
And quickly left my side;
I knew then she was lost to me,
To the sea she was a willing bride.
So she turned to catch the wave,
That took her to another shore;
Such a mermaid I never caught,
In my net before.

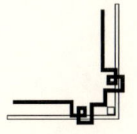

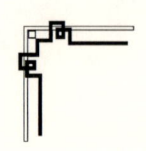

Between You and Me

When you are here
All hopes, dreams and ambitions disappear;
Drowned in your eyes when I hold your hand,
Unremembered now that I understand.
For you perplex my mind with memories
Of so many forgotten ecstasies;
Which were, are not and perhaps will never be
When we hold this moment between you and me.

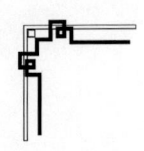

What Was Taken

We do not ask for retribution,
We try not cry with fear;
But we speak to all the men,
Who don't have ears to hear.
We cried to them again,
But no one heard our prayer;
We asked them for some mercy,
But no one ventured there.
Ours was the brook and meadow,
We held the scented flowers;
We had all to give to you,
To share the sunshine hours.
But these have be taken from us,
There's nothing left to save;
There's no wood for a table,
There's no earth for our grave.
You took the brook and meadow,
You took the scented flowers;
And all that we have left,
Are sad and empty hours.

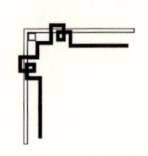

A Song

Too dear and elusive for pen or for word,
In verse unwritten or songs unheard;
As mysterious as the sounds of the sea,
Is that song my heart is singing to me.

At twilight with storm when all the trees shiver,
In the thunder of surf and rush on the river;
In the whisper of leaves and the fall of the rain,
I hear soft breezes coming back again.

From grey mists that cover the spinning of earth,
Out in the beyond where my spirit had birth;
From clouds over land and the fog of the sea,
Always forever their songs come to me.

There on the hilltop in beauty and light.
My soul like a bird in blue skies takes flight;
The pearly gates of heaven shine bright and near,
And the song in my heart is sweet and clear.

Up into realms where no human has trod,
Into time and infinity near to my God;
With brightness and stillness and all lovely things,
I'm brought where the voice of eternity sings.

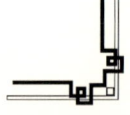

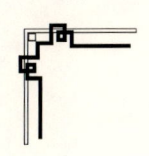

Life Is Good

Life is good and serene I sit,
For I never need to question it;
There's much I know that's odd no doubt,
But nature knows what it's all about.
Could things be different than they are
When all's in place from stone to star?
With thistledown that dips and flies,
With the wings of butterflies.

We try to feel the cosmic touch,
And know that we don't matter much;
A million stars up in the sky,
A million planets fall and die;
A million lives created you,
A million more have died for you.
Immortal we spend eternity,
With other lives we never see.

But sad to say don't blindly grope,
For lives we live beyond our hope;
With never death but ever change,
Eternal walk on earth to range.
With sorry lives we tell to all,
Of life's amazing carnival:
Just live the life that in you lies,
With love for life that never dies.

Life is good and serene I sit,
Loving every part of it;
I place my trust in my Father's plan,
And try to help him all I can;
And in a million years or so,
We'll know more than today we know.
So I'm glad to come and take my place,
Join hands with you and run the race.

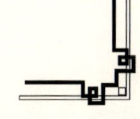

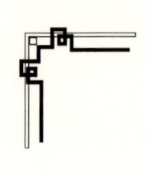

Resolution

Since trust is a mask that has nothing behind it
And hope is not found where mortal can find it;
Since love's looking glass can break in a minute
Catching the face that the soul has cast in it;
Why would we care for winters or springs
The scent of the blossom or the sweep of the wings?
Since all is for naught with good or for ill
Making folly an illusion to torment us still.

Since all the unrest and fervent endeavor
Is nothing but vanity now and forever;
A heart found bleeding to uphold the ideal
Is nothing but pride with nothing that's real.
Should a man be brave but not know the strife
With a reason to have and hold on to life?
Or die by the sword but not know the dare
Willing to be and be willing to bear?

Man knows now how fate may be cheated
How by being brave may the deeds be defeated;
Killing the longing that dies in your bosom
Desires not the fruit when you see the blossom;
Wish not for the flower when you think of the bud
Kill all the mavericks that cry for your blood.
Hopes unfulfilled are an illegal delight
For these are the dreams of a perfidious night;

So let me imagine an infinite peace
Felt without joy but a feeling of release;
Something by which an immortal decree
Is as like nothing as something can be.

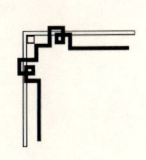

Some Men

Some love too little, some too long,
Some laugh and others cry;
Some do the act with show of tears
And some without a sigh;
Some men kill the things they love
Yet each man does deny.

Some kill love when in their youth,
And some when they grow old;
Some smother with the hand of greed
Because of lust for gold;
The evil use their tongue because
It takes love where it's cold.

Some men kill the girl they love
Have a story to be heard;
Some do it with a callous look
Some with a bitter word;
The tyrant does it with his fist
The coward with a sword.

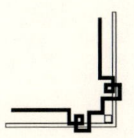

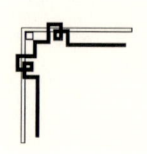

Way of the River

My waters had their genesis in the sea,
A path created was fashioned for me;
It can't be changed for there my toil
Bends through life in a twisting coil.
My waters end where they began,
Where life takes hold of its brief span;
To return to that enigmatic source,
Where once again I flow to on my course.
The fragrance from the flowers as I pass,
Scent the air with whispers from the grass;
And my waters run down as they go
Over gemlike stones my streamlets flow.
The tears that pour from my sad eyes,
Go back to the sea where all rivers rise;
And if my soul should suddenly leap
Over a ledge to kiss violets that sleep;
Then I will wander back to the sea,
The mother source that set me free.
And if those riddles I must keep,
Let me not complain, but sweep
On to the bitter end without fear,
Knowing that He who walks with me is near.

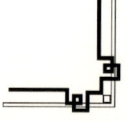

Destiny

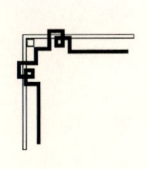

It's time to say good bye sly maid
It's futile and hopeless to regret you;
Neither faith nor memories give their aid
But pride will help me forget you.

For all these frivolous squandered years
The weary times of fading pleasures;
Your many loves, my ancient fears
The selfish songs of passion's treasures.

Had my destiny been joined with you
As at one time it appeared a token;
This folly would never have been true
And my heart would not be broken.

In times past my soul like yours was pure
And all its soaring passions would smother;
Now your promises no longer endure
You gave them to another.

Although now I look for other joys
For to see you would give me madness;
Alone among the crowds and hollow noise
I would concede to my heart's sadness.

At this time a thought would reveal
The sorrow in spite of hopeless endeavor;
My adversary might console all I feel
But I know you are gone from me forever.

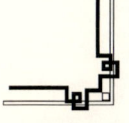

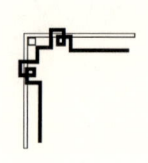

Is It Love

Is it love, this sweet unrest,
This yearning I feel within my breast?
For love has been lost for many a year,
It has gone, but I want love here.
Now it is time to make amends,
For love and I are meant to be friends.

But should I see you and touch your face,
And think awhile in this forlorn place;
Where in the silence I hear you sigh,
And touch your sorrow as you cry.
As you find and know my thought,
Forever dear, forget me not.

To find you through all the lonely pain,
Will bring to birth our love again;
For if we find it, should we turn away,
When it's true we are common clay?
Can life be fair, are we so fortunate,
That we should refuse the gift of fate?

The sudden wonder of longed for powers,
Has transformed all my worldly hours;
Our house is furnished, the pathway swept,
With all the lonely tears I wept;
Washed clean from endless fears,
From so many lost and lonely years.
Now lit with candles of hope at last,
To take away the darkness of the past.

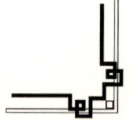

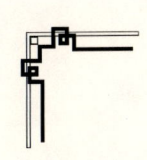

Why?

Dear love, can you tell me why
The dawn should be so pale
Or why the purple violet
Should shrivel in the vale?

Why does the lark that soars the sky
Should so sadly sing
And why from the hyacinth
The perfume of death should spring.

Why the sun that sails on high
So spitefully should frown;
And why my days so suddenly
Be sorrowful and brown.

Wy should I feel so forlorn
Need this come to be?
The days and nights are so long
Since you abandoned me.

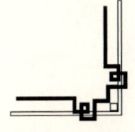

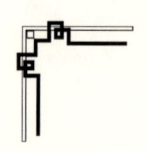

A Harvest

Look my love, across the pallid sand
And see the merging of sun and sea;
How they kiss beyond the land
And so shall we.

The sky's crimson harvest melts the sun
And the sea's pearls dissolve in the wine;
The sky drinks all but one
That one is mine.

Shine bright stars, soothe heaven's heart
Let the waves shimmer on dull sands;
Let the night break sun and sky apart
But not our lips or hands.

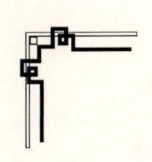

An Enigma

I lie all day beneath the tree,
Where fragrant branches shelter me;
I hear the groaning of its heart,
As the branches meet and part.

Like fingers laced and intertwined,
I hear the whisper in my mind;
Against the clouds wild geese fly,
Wings stretched out in the storm swept sky.

Back to their home they all have gone,
Their flight with hope leads them on;
Back to the land where they were born,
They fly with trust in the dawn of morn.

Home to the mist clad heather hill,
They fly the wind that carries them still;
And all the day I lie neath the tree,
Where power of flight is not given to me.

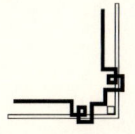

Sounds Of Summer

I heard the wind call out and say,
Arise my child, it's a brand new day;
School is out, it winds up with a sigh,
And the kids are dancing on feet that fly.

Flip flops and freckles burn in the sun,
Everyone is out there to soak up the fun;
The day is clear and the sky so blue,
Time to have fun and explore all that's new.

The bells on a truck roll up the street,
And we hear the patter of soft little feet;
The delicious taste of sweet ice cream,
Tickles the taste of a child's dream.

Sandcastles built for the waves to consume,
Shells to be found in the sands of the dune;
Racing and diving in foam topped waves,
Exploring and playing in cool dark caves.

Rollerskate downhill and double dutch rope,
A baseball game filled with hope;
Bubbles of pop that float up the nose,
A tasty hotdog, down the tummy it goes.

The meadow is loud with joyful noise,
With the carefree shouts of girls and boys;
The run with the grass between their toes,
To chase the sky where the butterfly goes.

There's lots to eat, all things delicious,
Bottoms to spank if the kids get officious;
But at the end of the day when all's said and done.
It was just perfect for all had such fun.

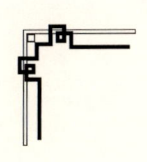

Always Love Me

A month of gentle loving May
With fields awake with flowers;
Out on the woodland path we play
In sunbeam's golden hours.
A hope that knows no fear,
Brings a kiss for you, a sigh at last;
When we felt that spell last year,
But now all that is past.

What a lovely world we knew
When dreams were bathed in pearly dew;
With brilliant fireflies all aglow
In wistful times of long ago.
When your eyes were wet with tears
For all the lost and lonely years;
With so many songs that lovers know
That you and I sang so long ago.

When the wind was on the river
And starlight danced where shadows shiver;
You took away the years of sorrow
And loved me more with each tomorrow.
So bring me hope and stars above me
And love me more but always love me.

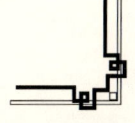

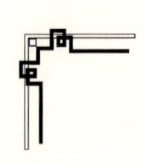

Caveat

They stood close at the garden gate,
In the fading of the sun;
There she might have known her fate,
By the little thing he'd done.

He picked a lovely flower,
He ripped it from its place;
In the twilight hour,
And touched it to his face.

He held the scented bloom,
In the midst of idle talk;
Then threw it down in the gloom,
In the dirt of the garden walk.

And then he trampled underfoot,
As it lay on the pathway there;
Then he scorned it with his boot,
For it was no longer fair.

'Twas then the lassie might have read,
The death of her life then;
But she looked into his eyes instead,
And saw her prince of men.

She kissed his mouth and blushed,
And felt the strength of his hold;
Then the fate of the flower crushed
Dispised, will once more be told.

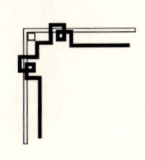

Beginnings and Endings

The words we are speaking in poesy,
Dance through the pages of history;
All the verses and all the rhymes,
Take all of us into more pensive times.
Where trickle of words that flow from pen,
Bring us from beginnings down to the end;
But in between there are stories to tell,
That can hold us all in a magic spell.
Portraits of birds looking their best,
Proudly sitting on eggs in a downy nest;
Tales of all the earth's funny creatures,
With so many faces, all different features.
Stories of a sun shining her light,
In a blue sky with clouds in flight;
Then there's another of a corpulent moon,
Skipping her moonbeams to a merry tune;
And armies of ants that travel in rows,
Carrying their bounty to where nobody knows;
Then there are people, all different shades,
Marching to music through life's parade.
So we can see that poems are a best friend,
They take us to beginnings that have no end.

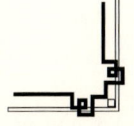

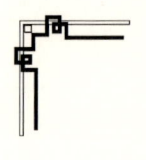

You Can

There is nothing at all in a person's dreams
Of a promise that won't come true;
Despite all the plotting and silly schemes
The dream is up to you.

Believe in yourself and the ability to find
Hopes found on rocky ground:
For all your dreams will prove in your mind
That hope for the spirit can be found.

When purpose is true and the mind is strong
There are no restraints to your power;
For strength behind pushes you along
And delivers a sweeter hour.

Whatever mountain your heart wants to climb
Though not scaled by another man;
If you will endure and take your time
Even if steep, you will know that you can.

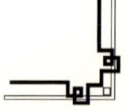

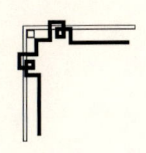

The Feast

You are as food and drink to my life
As showers give soul to the ground;
And for the joy to see you, the knife
Severs heart and soul without sound.
Yet, if my word should reach your ears
And you could know you are my treasure;
To drink all my yearning tears
I would love you without measure.
For my eyes delight on the face in my sight
And happy am I for that stare
From you who ignite all my dreams at night
And dissolve my inner being without care.
So I grieve and aspire each long day,
To feast on you if you would only come my way.

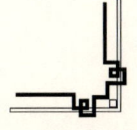

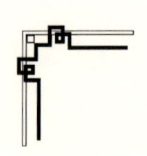

Wisdom

Laugh and the world laughs with you
Cry and you cry alone;
The natives of earth must steal their mirth
Or be sad and be on your own.
Speak and the mountains will call
Sigh and sound flies without care;
Echoes rebound with a mournful sound
As they float in the nebulous air.

Be happy and mankind will pursue you
Sorrow will drive them away;
They need the pleasure of all your leisure
But don't need your stories of grey.
Speak joy and your companions are many
With grief there's not many at all;
For there's nothing so fine as a sip of wine
But alone you will stumble and fall.

Celebrate and your table is gathered
Fast and the world will sigh;
Perfection to give will show how to live
But alone you must learn to die.
There is time in the soul for pleasure
There is space in the heart for rain;
But when it's begun look for the sun
Through the dark passage of pain.

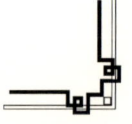

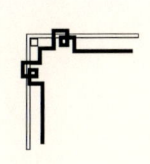

Belly Dancer

Another day is almost through,
Another day of missing you;
So I take myself to the cabaret,
To see you there as you swing and sway.

The lonely music filled the night,
I felt right then my heart take flight;
The voice that taunts behind the veil,
Haunting echoes that sob and wail.

Hips that glide with slow gyrations,
Arms that weave with undulations;
Languid eyes touched with kohl,
Whisper words to flame the soul.

The sounds of that persistent beat,
Soothe the brow with passion's heat;
Lost in the scene that ignites my eye,
Heats my skin and makes me cry.

You move thro night and cast your spell,
And thoughts I think I'll never tell.
Let's pretend there'll be no end,
For you are more to me than friend;

I want to take you in my arms,
And feel the warmth that never harms;
I play on the strings of love's romance,
As you swing and sway in a belly dance.

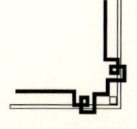

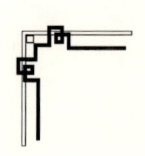

Done Deed

I come from a funeral
With tears they could see;
For I killed my lover
Who wouldn't love me.
His mouth with soft lips
That lit his sweet face
Brought a vision of sorrow
For a lonely grave's place.

For he did deceive me
And I couldn't find rest;
Till I turned and I slew him
Knowing this is best.
I stood there beside him
With a shovel in the clay;
Tomorrow I'll forget him
But I'll cry today.

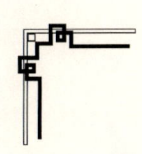

Separate Ways

I always wanted more
Than you were prepared to give;
It leads us now to separate ways
With altered lives to live.
My heart will always beat for you
With what little is left intact;
Love for you has come and gone
So now there's no turning back.
If you ever have a lonesome day
With nothing else to do;
Think back on our love filled days
When my love was all for you.